The Secret and SPIRITUALITY

The Secret and SPIRITUALITY

BILL L. LITTLE

DOVE INSPIRATIONAL PRESS
GRETNA 2008

Library of Congress Cataloging-in-Publication Data

Little, Bill L., 1935-
The secret and spirituality / by Bill L. Little.
p. cm.
ISBN 978-1-58980-591-0 (pbk. : alk. paper) 1. Success—Religious aspects—Christianity. 2. Christian life. 3. Byrne, Rhonda. Secret. 4. New Thought. I. Title.
BV4598.3.L58 2008
248.4—dc22
2008010018

Printed in the United States of America

Published by Dove Inspirational Press, an imprint of
Pelican Publishing Company, Inc.
1000 Burmaster Street, Gretna, Louisiana 70053

To Gay

Contents

Acknowledgments

Remembering and thanking all the people who have encouraged and assisted me in the production of this manuscript is almost impossible. I will name at least a few.

My wife Gay patiently read each chapter as I finished it. She edited and suggested clarification where it was needed. My friend Ed Viau also did a lot of proofreading and offered suggestions to make the manuscript stronger. Other friends, Tom Fletcher and Barbara Davis, patiently read, reread, and proofed the texts too.

Brian Mabry helped me to get the manuscript in final form on CDs, which was very important for me.

Jean Carnahan was especially helpful and spent a great deal of time helping me to formulate and clarify ideas shared in this manuscript. I express my thanks to her here.

I really appreciate Pelican Publishing Company for giving me the chance to get this material published. Special thanks go to Dr. Milburn Calhoun, President and Publisher of Pelican Publishing Company, and to Nina Kooij, Editor in Chief at Pelican.

Introduction

I was fascinated with the book *The Secret* when I discovered it soon after it was published in 2007. It was fascinating to me because I had used so many of the principles taught in the book. I had some questions about the scope and claims of the book. They seemed to me to be overstated and often inconsistent with things that I consider personal values.

I decided to compare the principles taught in *The Secret* with principles that seem to me to be spiritually sound and healthy.

This task necessitated broadening some of my spiritual ideas and narrowing some of the principles promoted in *The Secret.* I know there will be people who feel that I am being too restrictive in my views of *The Secret* and others who will feel that I am not being strict enough in my spiritual guidelines. It is the old problem of appearing in the middle of a Civil War battle wearing gray pants and a blue coat. Doing so is likely to bring shots from both sides.

I hope I have been fair in my evaluation and reactions. That is important to me because I hope to influence many who would be reluctant to embrace concepts in *The Secret* because they are "New Age" ideas. It seems to me a shame that people miss so much in life because they restrict themselves from drawing what is good from philosophies with which they disagree.

I hope this material will open doors for many people who would otherwise have missed opportunities for personal growth, achievement, and even material acquisitions. At any rate I ask you the reader to consider it with an open mind.

The *Secret* and SPIRITUALITY

1

A Quick Look at *The Secret*

My father gave me the key to everything that was important in life. The problem was that he kept giving me different keys. He once said, "Bill, the key to everything is flexibility. If you are flexible you can always adjust to any job or situation in life." Later he told me, "Bill, the key to everything is a sense of humor. If you have a good sense of humor you will always be able to get by." Again he said, "Bill, the key to everything is humility. You will never have a problem learning a job if you have enough humility to ask questions." All were small "keys" but not the "master key."

Because we are all looking for the "master key" to unlock the mysteries of life, there has been much interest in a recent book titled *The Secret.* The author, Rhonda Byrne, says that "the secret to everything" is "attraction." Attraction is achieved through our thoughts and feelings, which, in turn, produce the desires of our heart.

So if we want something, we are advised to think clearly about it and get a sense or feeling of what it would be like if we had it, visualize receiving it, and simply ask for it.

Since we acquire or achieve the things we think about (good or bad), it is certainly best to veer toward the positive and the best. This might explain why

Debby Downer, one of the fictional characters on the *Saturday Night Live* TV show, is such a pathetic loser who always feeds herself and others with negative thoughts. According to *The Secret,* the dread of trouble actually attracts it into our life like metal shavings to a magnet. Since likes attract, our mental field becomes a lodestone for negative energy. But if we think about and focus on positive things, then that is what we will receive. This principle is consistent with the comment by the writer of Proverbs thousands of years ago, "As he [a person] thinks in his heart, so is he" (Proverbs 23:7).

The principle is said to apply to people and situations as well as to material things. A situation that we visualize is likely to materialize. We will more likely attract the type of people we think about and want in our life. Our evolving positive thoughts will keep away negative thinking, as well as negative people.

Valid Laws Apply to All

The law of attraction is a valid law. It operates in the lives of Christians, agnostics, atheists, Buddhists, and Mohammedans alike. It operates because it is true. I don't know why that is a hard concept to accept, but it seems to be for some people.

The Christian Scriptures teach that we reap whatever we sow (Galatians 6:7-8). If we sow negative thoughts and visions, we will attract negative things. If we sow thoughts and visions of sickness, we will attract sickness. If we sow thoughts and visions of health, we will attract wellness.

Thoughts Create Reality

It doesn't matter who discovers or promotes a truth, it remains true for everyone. If an unbeliever had discovered the law of gravity it would nevertheless be true for believers as well. If a Buddhist discovered a cure for any disease, it would be a cure for Christians, Mohammedans, atheists, and all others. It simply does not matter who discovers truth; it is truth because it is true.

I really like what Michael Bernard Beckwith is quoted as saying in *The Secret.* "We live in a universe in which there are laws, just as there is a law of gravity. If you fall off a building it doesn't matter if you're a good person or a bad person, you're going to hit the ground" (p. 27). He then points out that the law of attraction is a law of nature and is as impartial and impersonal as the law of gravity.

It Has Been Long Known

It has long been known that we create much of our reality by the thoughts we feed our mind, just as we create our physical health by the food we feed our body. "Peace of mind and a healthy body are inevitable when you begin to think and feel in the right way. Whatever you claim mentally and feel as true, your subconscious mind will accept and bring forth" (Murphy, p. 30). Too many of us get into the habit of filling our mind with "junk food," that is, thoughts that have no positive mental health value.

We may say negative things to ourselves like, "I am prone to sickness. I am clumsy. I never seem to do anything right. I can't control my weight. I am always late for appointments." Just imagine what a steady diet of such thoughts produces over time: stress, lack of confidence, defeatism, hopelessness, and illness.

We can just as easily say positive things to ourselves. We can say, "I am unusually healthy. I seem to be agile. I do most things right. I eat what is good for me. I make it a point to be on time for my appointments."

These positive assertions are filed away in our "thought folders" much like a stored document on a computer. Later when we do mental searches on a related topic or situation, the appropriate, or inappropriate, thought is loaded onto our mental screen. As the old computer saying goes, "Garbage in, garbage out." What flashes up on our mental screen determines how we perform, what we say, and what we become. Our thoughts attract and reinforce the behaviors or circumstances they describe.

John Maxwell in his book *21 Indispensable Qualities of a Leader* wrote: "What you think means more than anything else in your life: more than what you earn; more than where you live; more than your social position, and more than what anyone else may think about you."

Yes, there is incredible power within us waiting like dormant batteries to be charged up and put to use. If it is true that our thoughts and feelings attract things, people, and circumstances that create our reality, then we are responsible for the things in our life, the people in our life, and the circumstances of our life. Even if this is only partially true, it is tremendously important for us to know and to control.

Thoughts generate emotion, and emotion has a powerful effect on our outlook and sense of purpose. If we wake up in the morning excited about the day's activities, we will feel a lot more creative and energized than if we are dreading the day.

If we are going to do something enjoyable, like playing a round of golf, we spring out of bed with far more pep than we do if we have something disagreeable to do, like keeping an appointment with the IRS. When we stimulate our thinking with energy-enhancing messages, we sense a surge of vitality that will pick us up and carry us through the day.

This is fantastically good news, you are thinking, if it is actually true. You can improve your lot in life by taking charge of your thoughts and feelings. At last you can get the things you want in life, increase your achievements, and control your relationships.

But let's look at this "have it all under all circumstances" scenario from a Christian perspective. Is this nothing more than the televangelists' "name it and claim it" promise?

A Disclaimer

Note that when I compare Christian teachings to the teachings of The Secret, *I am not referring to the teachings of Christian "prosperity televangelists" who promise prosperity to those who support them with sacrificial gifts.*

Many of these televangelists take an approach to Christian faith that emphasizes what is called "the prosperity gospel." This approach proclaims that if we obey the "laws" of prosperity, think right, live right, and, of course contribute support to their "ministries," God will give us great abundance in our life. I am certain this brand of prosperity theology is in conflict with the teachings of Jesus. There are some similarities between the teachings of these prophets of prosperity and the teachers of *The Secret.* But they are certainly not the same.

The teachers of *The Secret* do not claim to promote its concepts in the name of God; they do not ask for contributions to their programs, nor do I sense any attempt to instill guilt in the people to whom they communicate. I believe that most of the televangelists, while perhaps sincere and well-intended, are misguided in their attempts to promote prosperity to everyone.

The Christian, buried to self by faith, is forced to confront limitations. Self is no longer the primary motivator or consideration. The Christian must ponder the effect that his wants, deeds, and even thoughts will have on others. There are some obvious limitations. For example, we may want very much another person's spouse, yacht, or house, or a coworker's job. So, in order to use *The Secret* wisely there must be some guardrails built around our mind. That, I believe, is a necessary discipline, and one that is described in this book.

2

How I Have Applied *The Secret* in My Life

Before looking at the discipline called guardrails of the mind, I want to share with you how I have used concepts that are now called *The Secret.* I believe you will see that I clearly embrace some of the basic concepts and find no conflict between them and my own Christian faith.

Some of our discoveries are serendipitous. They just seem to happen, or as the teachers of *The Secret* would say, "They are attracted to us." Whether the ideas I am describing in this book were attracted to my mind or not, I cannot say. I didn't even know that I knew them. I just knew.

I was thirteen years old at the time and daydreamed a lot, even at times lived in a fantasy world. For some reason I started drawing pictures of my dreams. I now know that those drawings were images of my goals, my deep desires, and I was visualizing the fulfillment of them. The pictures I drew were crude, but they were physical images of specific dreams being fulfilled.

After a recent move and while rummaging through some old boxes I came across the little notebook, a small brown leather-covered spiral notebook. I had forgotten the pictures and had not looked at them since my freshman year in high school, and I was now finished with graduate school and a grandfather. It was thrilling to see the drawings. Let me describe them to you.

Dreams Fulfilled

I drew a picture of myself scoring the winning goal in a basketball game and breaking the school scoring record. The picture showed the fans and cheerleaders in the background, and there was a caption over them, "Yea, Little!"

When I was a senior in high school, that scene was actually repeated several times, and I set the scoring record, broke it, and set a new one, three times. The only difference in the actual experience and the picture was in the kind of shot that was made to win the game and set the record. The picture was of a driving layup, but the experience was actually a jump shot. But it came true!

The second picture was of me, standing in front of the school assembly, thanking my classmates for electing me as president of the student body. That was a stretch for a poor farm boy, but anyone can dream. I even wrote the total votes over the picture. In my imagination, the winning number of votes was 255.

At the end of my junior year I was elected president of the student body, and the vote count was very close to my vision. The winning number of votes was 252 on the first ballot. The vision came true!

A third picture was of a colleague and me winning a debate. At that time I really knew nothing about debate, but I had sat in on a debate, and it looked interesting. During my senior year, my colleague and I won many debates and even made it to the state regional debate tournament finals. The vision came true!

I also drew a picture of myself flying an airplane. It was an open cockpit plane. The planes that I actually flew were not open cockpit planes, but I did fly. I flew several different aircraft until I grew tired of the hassle of renting planes and dealing with traffic over St. Louis and quit flying several years ago. The amazing point is that the vision came true!

There was one picture of me standing behind the pulpit of a church. I don't know where that came from. I was not really thinking in that direction. I planned to be an engineer, as did about a third of the graduating class. Most of us didn't go that route, but I did find myself behind the pulpit of a church. I have served as pastor of one church for forty-eight years. Even that image became a reality.

Partial Fulfillment

There were other pictures, but this gives you the idea. In all honesty, there was one picture that did not come true. I drew a picture of myself in a St. Louis Cardinal uniform, playing in the Cardinal outfield. I never played baseball. It was not a sport at our high school in Southeast Missouri. So that did not happen, but I did work for the Cardinals as their team psychologist. Once when I was running in the outfield with some of the players and playing catch during spring training, I thought, "This is close enough!"

Not only did my experience with the baseball Cardinals coincide with some of the basic teachings in *The Secret,* it verifies the contention that we don't have to know how our goals are going to be fulfilled. I had no idea of how, but I knew that I wanted to work with that team. This is how it happened:

In the late 1970s I started thinking about what a

thrill it would be to work with professional baseball players. One night my wife and I with two friends were driving downtown in St. Louis. As we drove past the baseball stadium, I said to the group, "I think I will become a team psychologist for the Cardinals." One of the friends said, "They are not going to let you mess with the minds of those highly paid players."

I said, "I believe they will." I did not know how that would come about, but I believed that it would. At the time I had been working with cancer patients using visualization. Somehow, one of the players, a relief pitcher who had pitched for the Kansas City Royals, found out about my work. He called and asked if I would work with him, using visualization. I said that I would. He told other players about our sessions, and soon several players were seeking time for me to help them with various needs, personally and professionally.

The relief pitcher appeared in seventy-nine games that year. It was a club record. He had one of the lowest runs per inning statistics in the league. Other pitchers, especially minor leaguers, asked if I would use the techniques to help them. I did. The players, including some established players, asked for help. They were vocal about the help I gave them.

The manager of the Cardinals asked me to work with the whole club that year, 1982. I had already been to spring training with the team for the previous two years, and it was certainly not a difficult decision for me. Of course I would. It was one of the most enjoyable experiences of my life, and I believe I helped a number of the players that year to stay focused, deal with personal problems, and improve specific skills. The only disappointment came when the manager would not permit me in the clubhouse during the World Series. I missed out on the conclusion of that season, but nothing takes away from the overall joy I experienced.

It was difficult for me to understand the way it ended, but soon I understood that even that ending was not all bad. Several articles were written about my work and not long afterward another team asked me to work with them. I did that for the next four years. What a great experience, and I believe it all came into existence because of thoughts, vision, believing, and acting when the time came.

Goal Setting

I believe in setting goals, specific goals. I still draw pictures of my goals. I see myself sitting behind a stack of books in a bookstore. I am signing them. The book has a colorful cover and is titled *The Secret and Spirituality.* If you are reading this message from a book, then that dream has come true.

It is exciting to share these stories, and one more story is very important to me. It has to do with my work with cancer patients. Again, I did not know how, but I knew that I wanted to make a contribution to the treatment of cancer patients. This is how that happened.

From the time I began to work on my PhD dissertation, I dreamed of using the principles I was researching in working with cancer patients. I did not know how that was going to be brought about, but I dreamed of doing it.

I discussed it with my wife Gay. We started formalizing a plan. It involved talking with some community leaders who might help us raise funds to begin a program that would provide state of the art support for cancer patients and their families but without charge to the patients.

One of the men with whom we talked was especially interested. His wife had cancer. He asked if I would work with her. I was happy to do so and had a wonderful experience giving support to her and her family. He became one of our original board members.

Other board members came from cancer patients we were able to help and from members of their families. Soon we had enough support to open the Cancer Support Center of St. Louis. Over the next ten years we saw more than fifteen hundred cancer patients and many of their families. The only thing that stopped our work was that after ten years, hospitals began to add support programs to their treatment regimens through building "centers of excellence." We were even invited to share what we had learned by meeting with one large hospital's planning committee. This development reduced the need for what we were doing.

There is no way of knowing for sure, but I believe we influenced the medical community to broaden its treatment scope. That was a fulfillment of our dream, and out of it two of my books were published, *Help Yourself Heal,* and *Prevention: The Ultimate Cure.* I certainly have enjoyed and benefited from the basic concepts of the material contained in *The Secret,* even years before I read the book.

Thankfully, not all my dreams have come true. Some of them would have been unfortunate for me. The topic of failed dreams will be dealt with in chapter 6 on "Major Issues for Christians in *The Secret.*"

I believe that if we ask for what we desire, seek to know if it is right for us, and then go forward as if it will happen, it will happen. Note that there is a condition in my conclusion, "if it is right for us." That is an issue with which Christians are concerned. That issue is further discussed in the next chapter, which is devoted to parallels and differences between what Christ taught and what the proponents of *The Secret* teach.

3

The Secret Versus The Sacred

There are many similarities between the teachings of Jesus and the teachings of *The Secret,* but there are some differences as well. Application of the general principles taught in *The Secret* will probably make life better for most anyone. I urge people to read them, and decide which of them they want to apply to their life.

It is also true that applying the teachings of Jesus Christ will certainly make anyone's life better. There are many similarities with *The Secret,* but there are also some glaring differences. A fundamental difference is in the added focus by Christians on what happens as a result of our values when this life is over. This focus influences and, in some instances limits, our application of the principles taught in *The Secret.*

We are faced with the reality that even the most positive-thinking, positive-visualizing, good-feeling, grateful, faithful people will have some difficulties in life, and they will ultimately come to the end of life. What then? I did not find the answer to that question in *The Secret.*

Now let's examine some of the principles of *The Secret* to see how they compare with the principles of Christian teaching. Hereafter I will refer to this comparison thus: *The Secret* versus The Sacred.

The Principle of Judgment

The Secret

One difference between Christian thought and some of the material in *The Secret* lies in the statement by Neale Donald Walsch, "So your purpose is what you say it is. Your mission is the mission you give yourself. Your life will be what you create it as, and no one will stand in judgment of it, now or ever" (p. 177).

The Sacred

The problem with this principle for Christians is that we believe we will be judged. The writer of Hebrews summed it up in these words: "It is appointed unto men once to die, but after this the judgment" (Hebrews 9:27 KJV). Paul adds, "We must all appear before the judgment seat of Christ" (2 Corinthians 5:10). Christians are unable to ignore this fact, even if we embrace and apply the vast majority of the teachings of *The Secret.*

Here are some more of the basic principles from *The Secret* with parallels and some shades of difference between them and most Christian thought.

The Principle of Attraction

The Secret

Simply stated by Bob Proctor, "The Secret is the law of attraction!" (p. 4). John Assaraf adds, "The simplest way for me to look at the law of attraction is if I think of myself as a magnet, and I know that a magnet will attract to it" (p. 7). Dr. Joe Vitale notes, "Thoughts are sending out that magnetic signal that is drawing the parallel back to you" (p. 10).

Attraction is a result of thoughts, imagination (visualization), goal setting, feelings, and focus in our life. You, no doubt, know several people who think about, talk about, and describe in detail their pain and misfortunes. Trust me when I tell you that their lives are filled with pain and misfortune. Even when something good happens they cannot enjoy it because they are still expecting the next catastrophe.

You probably also know many other people who think about, talk about, and describe the joys and good times in their lives. Their lives are generally filled with joy and good times. Even when something bad happens to them, they are not overwhelmed because they are still expecting something good to come out of it. They are trusting in the promise of Romans 8:28, "We know that all things work together for good to those who love God."

The Sacred

There is one hazy area surrounding the teachings on the principle of attraction. The basic law of attraction is that we, through our thoughts, feelings, visualizations, and desires, draw into our life things that are consistent with all of those thoughts, feelings, visualizations, and desires. The law is stated in terms leading to the conclusion that whatever comes into our life or whatever happens to us was drawn to us by our own focus. I have already indicated that I believe there is a lot to be learned and applied from this principle. There is tremendous truth in that concept, but there is a caution to be noted: *Don't push it too far.*

In *The Secret* Dr. Joe Vitale puts his finger on the problem for me when he says, "Everything that surrounds you right now in your life, including the things you're complaining about, you've attracted. Now I know at first blush that's going to be something that you hate to hear" (p. 27). He is consistent in insisting that this is true. The summary statement is, "Nothing can come into your experience unless you summon it through persistent thoughts" (p. 28). Most truth can be pushed too far. Any truth pushed to the extreme can become a lie. Concerning attraction we should note that it is not one hundred percent true that we draw all of our experiences to ourselves. Some things come as a result of what people around us are doing, thinking, and visualizing.

Christians are confronted with the question that the disciples asked Jesus, "Who sinned, this man or his parents, that he was born blind" (John 9:2). They assumed that there had to be a connection between sin and the blindness just as one might press the idea that it was attracted to him, perhaps through the negative thoughts of his parents. Jesus said that it was neither; it was a situation that permitted the power of God to be revealed and was no one's fault (v. 3).

Christians offer a word of encouragement to the starving, the blind, the deaf, the cancer ridden, the dying, and otherwise suffering people: *It is not necessarily your fault!* Yes, you can make your situation better and more livable by applying the principles of *The Secret,* but that does not mean that all your suffering will end. It does mean that your life will be better.

It is also true that you can make your pain worse by focusing on it, thinking about it, and talking about it incessantly, but it may not end, even with your most faith-filled moments. Still you will be better off to apply every positive principle you can find. Focus on attracting hope. Never give up hope. Remember that there is no such thing as false hope. There is only hope.

The Principle of Abundance

The Secret

"There is enough [in the universe] for everyone," thus says Michael Bernard Beckwith, one of the teachers of *The Secret* (p. 150). Rhonda Byrne adds on the same page, "There is an abundance of all things . . . . There is an unlimited supply." Later in the book Dr. Joe Vitale states: "There is more than enough in the Universe. . . . We can create it any way we want it, by using the law of attraction" (p. 167).

The Sacred

Christian teaching includes the idea of abundance. Jesus said that He came that we might have life and have it more abundantly (John 10:10). The Scriptures teach that God is able to do abundantly more than we expect (Ephesians 3:20). In Psalm 51:10, the psalmist says that the cattle on a thousand hills belong to God. I know this verse because my grandmother often quoted it to me when times were hard. She wasn't worried because she knew that God had abundance and could always take care of us.

In the Sermon on the Mount (Matthew 5-7), Jesus taught that we do not need to worry about what we will wear or eat because the Father knows that we need these things and will provide them for us (Matthew 6:32-33). In order to get the point across He pointed to the birds that, though they do not work, still have plenty to eat, and then to the lilies of the field and how they were clothed even better than was King Solomon in all of his splendor (vv. 26-28).

Christians believe in the abundance of things, but we also believe in stewardship. We believe that we are to exercise care for the abundance of nature. We are to use what we have been given wisely. To do otherwise is to contribute to the growing environmental problems of the world.

The Principle of Asking

The Secret

Both Christian teaching and *The Secret* emphasize asking for what we want. Teachers of *The Secret* say that we are to ask the universe. One, James Ray (pp. 45-46), says the universe is like the genie from Aladdin's lamp who is always asking us, "What do you wish?" When we make clear what we want, the universe provides it for us.

The Sacred

Christians also teach that we are to ask for the things we want. Jesus instructed that we do so (Luke 11:1-13). While others suggest that it doesn't matter what we call the one or the thing to which we are praying, Christians believe it does make a difference. That difference is more than semantics. Praying to God involves seeking to please Him even in our asking. We don't have to worry about pleasing the universe, just ask for anything that pleases God.

The book of James says, in agreement with *The Secret,* that the reason we do not have is because we do not ask. James goes on to add that we can ask and not receive if we ask for the wrong motives in order to spend what we receive on our own pleasures (James 4:3). Christians are concerned with motives. When the motives are not selfish, we can ask and receive. Jesus said, "Ask, and it will be given to you; seek, and you will find; knock, and it will be opened to you" (Matthew 7:7).

Both emphasize asking, but Christian teaching adds the limitation of motive to the asking.

Both focus on the fact that we grow faith by beginning to ask for things that we can really trust in. A prayer that I often pray is, "God, bring into my life the right things, the right people, and the right ideas at the right time and in the right way." That is not a bad way to begin asking. I learned to ask for these things at least forty years ago and have enjoyed receiving the answers to my prayers many times.

The proponents of *The Secret* say that the first thing we must do in order to attract the things we want is "ask." They are saying that we simply ask the universe. For the Christian, asking is prayer. As Christians, we ask God for the things we desire and trust Him to answer our prayers in accordance with His will.

The Principle of Alignment

The Secret

The Secret says that we are to bring ourselves into

alignment with the universe. We are told to focus on its abundance, believe it will give us what we ask, and then be positive and receive.

The Sacred

Christians believe that we are to bring our lives into alignment with the will of God. In fact, many of us believe that the primary purpose of prayer (asking) is that we may conform to what we understand to be God's desires for us. The model for that prayer is found in the Garden of Gethsemane (Matthew 26:36-46) where Jesus prayed to His Father in heaven, "Not as I will, but as You will" (v. 39). That is the highest level of Christian praying.

Basically the difference is in with what or with whom we are to bring ourselves into alignment, but there is no question about the power of alignment. When our conscious mind and our subconscious mind are aligned, we are totally focused. When an athlete is focused internally as well as externally he is said to be "in the zone." There is no higher level of performance for an athlete than being "in the zone." We Christians always seek to pray "in the zone."

The Secret sees great power in being aligned with the universe. I cannot argue with that principle, and do not wish to. I would just point out that for the Christian the desired alignment is with God. If we are in alignment with God, we will be in alignment with the universe. We believe that if we bring together our subconscious mind and our conscious mind with the will of God, He is then able to release through our life miracle-working power.

Christian teaching further notes that when two or more people are in alignment with God and with each other, Jesus says that they can ask what they will and it will be done (Matthew 18:19; John 15:3 KJV). That is even greater Power than the power of *The Secret.*

The Principle of Faith or Believing

The Secret

According to Lisa Nichols in the *The Secret,* after asking for whatever is desired, "Step two is believe. Believe that it's already yours. Have what I call unwavering faith. Believing in the unseen" (p. 48). The order is ask and then believe.

The Sacred

Christians certainly have no difference with this general principle. Our approach is summed up in Matthew 21:22 NIV, "If you believe, you will receive whatever you ask for in prayer." Perhaps an even more clear statement is found in Mark 11:24 NIV, "Therefore I tell you, whatever you ask for in prayer, believe that you have received it, and it will be yours."

Faith is what we *really* believe, not what we say we believe. Often people really want to believe and try to believe, they just don't. Trying is not the same as believing. Wanting to believe is fine, but it is not the same as believing. We cannot muster up faith like Alice in Wonderland, by closing our eyes and trying harder. Faith begins with honesty. We must start where we really are with what we honestly and deeply believe and build from there.

I worked for several months with a cancer patient who tried hard to believe that she was going to beat the cancer. I wanted her to begin with a belief that it was possible to beat the cancer. That seemed to be a faith-sized request. She said that she believed it was possible.

Perhaps she wanted to please me, or perhaps she had fooled herself, but either way she told me one day that she really believed that she had beaten the cancer. I asked her how long she thought she would live. She was in her early sixties at the time. She said she thought she would make it about five more years. I said, "And then, how do you think you will die?"

She did not hesitate, "From cancer."

She did not really believe she had beaten the cancer, but she wanted to believe it. It was not what she said she believed that mattered. It was what she really believed that mattered. It is possible to build faith, but only if we are honest about where we are at the present.

Another more mundane, but clear example of the strength of internal belief systems comes from my years of working with baseball players. I often told players that "no one performs consistently at a level that is inconsistent with his real beliefs." Many of them bought into that concept and worked on their belief systems in order to bring about permanent change in their performance levels.

One player clearly believed that he was a .300 hitter. That, as baseball fans know, is not bad. He had such a great swing and great eye-hand coordination that I believed he could be an even better hitter. I worked with him for two months. I repeatedly told him that he could hit .340 or .350. I even made an audiotape with that input on it. He said he listened to it.

By midseason he was hitting near .340. I overheard a reporter interviewing him in the clubhouse. The reporter said he had seen me working with him and wondered what I had been saying. The player said I had been telling him that he could hit for a higher average, perhaps .340 or .350.

The reporter responded, "I believe that is right. You do have a very good swing, and you seem to see the ball well." I listened intently. It was good to have a second person giving him the same input. The reporter continued, "So, what do you think you will hit this season?"

The player did not pause to think. He simply said, ".300." That is exactly the average he had at the end of the season. It did not matter what he wanted to believe. He still believed the old message that he had been sending himself throughout his entire career. His career average was .300.

Faith cannot be faked. An old Alcoholics Anonymous adage is, "Fake it until you can make it." That is a helpful concept, but it is only a first step. It can help in the short run, but in the long run our deepest and strongest beliefs influence our performance in life. The hope is that through "faking it," or starting with what little faith we have, we will be able to grow into more faith. Like the man who came to Jesus with a desperate need, we say, "Lord, I believe; help my unbelief!" (Mark 9:24).

As noted above, we agree with the concept taught in *The Secret* concerning starting small. "Starting with something small, like a cup of coffee or parking spaces, is an easy way to experience the law of attraction in action" (p. 69). If we begin and frequently practice asking for the things that we really do believe will come true, we build our faith muscles and gradually believe in bigger and better things. This is true of Christian faith in God and His power, as well as faith in the basic laws of the universe. In fact, the whole Christian life is grounded in the concept of starting where we are and growing from there. The challenge is, "Accept as much of God as we understand in Jesus Christ, and accept more as we understand more."

Making faith-sized requests that help us build stronger faith is consistent with the tool used in behavior modification for years. It is called "small approximations." One application of this principle is seen in classrooms where children are rewarded, not for perfect behavior, but for improved behavior.

This concept is seen most clearly in the way we give feedback to our children. When a child takes a first step, we gleefully proclaim that the child is walking. That is not entirely true. One step is not walking, but it is a small approximation of walking, and we reward it with smiles, hugs, and words of encouragement. The result of rewarding a small approximation is that it leads to bigger achievements.

Writers use the same concept when writing a book. A book begins with a small approximation, a word, a sentence, a paragraph, and then a page.

Faith grows in the same way. We ask for things that we can honestly believe, and then build on that foundation. As we see those "small" requests fulfilled, we move on to greater requests with increasing faith. So begin where you are, with what you can believe. Your faith will grow if you exercise it.

The Principle of Gratitude

The Secret

Basically there is agreement on the high priority of gratitude. We must express thanks for what we have and what we desire. Paul told the Philippians to make their requests known to God with thanksgiving (Philippians 4:6).

Few would question the value of starting every day with expressions of gratitude. One writer in *The Secret* told of putting a small rock in his pocket to remind him of gratitude. When he put his hand into his pocket to get change, he would feel the rock and remember to give thanks. We all need reminders to be grateful, and this is a wonderful one. A small rock placed in our pocket can be a constant reminder to express thanks.

I connect bowing to prayers of thanksgiving. I bow down, or bend over, to dry my feet after a shower. That is a cue for me to remember to express gratitude for all the wonderful things in my life: my family, my health, my opportunities (past, present, and future), and every expression of love I give and receive. When I do exercises and touch my toes, I again offer prayers of thanksgiving. Use whatever will help you to remember to be thankful.

The Sacred

The major difference between *The Secret* and Christian teaching is in the object of our thanksgiving.

People who teach *The Secret* say that we are to express gratitude. They do not say to whom or to what we are to express it, simply that we are to express it. Christians believe that we are to give thanks to God for all that He is and for all that we receive from Him. He is the source of all life.

The Principle of Joy

The Secret

"Laughter attracts joy, releases negativity, and leads to miraculous cures" (p. 139). Again, Neale Donald Walsch says, "Joy, love, freedom, happiness, laughter. That's what it is. And if you just experience joy sitting there and meditating for an hour, by golly, do that" (p. 178).

The Sacred

There is much agreement with this principle in Christian values. The Scriptures are filled with comments on joy, gladness, rejoicing, and happiness. Paul wrote to the Philippians, "Rejoice . . . again I say, Rejoice" (Philippians 4:4 KJV). Jesus said that He had come so that He might leave His joy with us and that our joy might be complete (John 15:11 NIV). The writer of the book of Proverbs said that a merry heart has healing power (Proverbs 17:22 NIV). The psalms are filled with thoughts of joy and gladness. Jesus and His disciples enjoyed parties. I love joy and laughter. My personal desire is for Christians along with everyone else to focus more on love and joy.

We have a right to have as much fun as we can. Fun

and humor in general is healthy. That is no longer a point that needs research. Dr. Joe Vitale in *The Secret* says, "You want to become aware of your thoughts and choose your thoughts carefully and you want to have fun with this" (p. 23).

This is such an overlooked value among Christians that special emphasis is made on it in the following paragraphs.

Humor and Spirituality

> "Joy is the infallible sign of the presence of God."
>
> (Teilhard de Chardin)

I love humor. Even a little bit of it brightens my day. I got more than a flicker of light from these statements:

"Does the name Pavlov ring a bell?"

"I used to think I was indecisive, but now I'm not sure."

"What if there were no hypothetical questions?"

Those are examples of Stephen Wright's humor. A similar mind-set to his is found in this next suggestion for reducing stress:

"Make a list of things you have already done."

Or how about, "Call the psychic hotline and just say, 'Guess who?'"

Warning on a Japanese food processor: "Not to be used for the other use."

Warning on the packet containing a Chinese tin opener: "Similar to items seen on TV." My wife will want one of those!

Why Laugh?

"The most acutely suffering animal on earth invented laughter." (Friedrich Nietzsche)

I have always loved to laugh, but I didn't realize how important it was until I learned some of the following principles:

1. Laugh because it is healthy.

In recent years we have learned of the healing value of humor. Norman Cousins influenced us tremendously with his use of Marx Brothers' films to cure himself of what was considered an incurable disease. We have learned that there are a number of benefits from laughter.

The book of Proverbs teaches that, "A merry heart does good, like medicine" (17:22).

Laughing increases antibodies in saliva that combat upper respiratory infections.

Laughing decreases serum cortical, and in so doing becomes an antidote for the harmful effects of stress.

Laughing causes the body to secrete an enzyme that protects the stomach from forming ulcers.

Laughing conditions and tones the abdominal muscles.

Laughing changes the perspective.

Laughing just plain feels good.

Laughing generates more positive mental attitudes.

Laughing improves ventilation and thereby helps reduce negative respiratory conditions.

Laughing frees interleukin-2 and other immune boosters in the body.

Laughing releases endorphins, which provide natural pain relief.

Laughing helps in the flow of oxygen throughout the body.

Since it is true that humor enables us to reduce the effects of stress, it helps us deal with one of the major health and mental problems that we face. Surely humor helps us to live effective lives. In fact, I do not believe we can live a consistently high-quality life without humor.

I'm glad I have developed the skill of having fun. My sense of humor is my seventh sense. Because of it, I tell my friends that they will be hard pressed to find me having a bad day.

2. Laugh because it reduces fatigue.

Years ago I read a book titled *How Never to Be Tired.* The major premise of the book was that having fun reduces fatigue. If we enjoy doing something, we are much less likely to feel tired than if we are doing something we dread. Note the comparison above between days of pleasure and those of dread.

I can feel literally worn out and be asked to go to the gym to shoot a few baskets. That invitation energizes me. I almost always feel like having fun. If I am getting up in the morning to go on an exciting outing with friends or family, or to do something else enjoyable, I am much more eager to get going than I would be if I were going to do something I dislike or don't want to do. Fun reduces fatigue.

3. Laugh because it is easier than a lot of other exercises. Norman Cousins reported that Dr. William Fry, Jr., of the Department of Psychiatry at Stanford Medical School says that laughter is a form of physical exercise. He asserts that twenty seconds of laughter can double the heart rate for three to five minutes. That is the equivalent of three minutes of strenuous rowing. As much as I love exercise I would rather laugh than row.

4. Laugh with (not at) your family because it will improve your personal relationships. If you do not learn to laugh you may discover what one somber man discovered. His home was his hassle. In fact Dostoevsky wrote in *The Adolescent* that one of the best ways to get to know a person is to watch the way he laughs. He suggested that young women should watch how a man laughs before they decide to marry him.

Christians should be the most joyful people in the world!

The Principle of Positive Input

The Secret

I doubt that many people have any trouble believing in the power of positive thoughts. Christians and all others would be wise to inundate themselves with as many positive thoughts as possible. The continuation of positive thinking will make any life better. Norman Vincent Peale surely opened our minds to this concept.

The Sacred

We feed our minds constantly. Why not feed it positive things and reap positive things? No matter what our religion, we are feeding our mind every minute of every day. An unusually perverse client sat in my office. I was trying to convince her to make some changes in her thought processes in order to help her feel better.

"You know that your mind and body are connected," I said as I began my lesson on the mind and body.

"Mine are not," she smirked.

"Well, maybe yours are not," I conceded.

"Oh, my brain and body are connected." I thought she was making a concession.

"Okay then, what goes into your brain?" I thought that remark would corner her.

She was almost gleeful in her response. "Nothing when I am comfortable."

There may be people who honestly believe that nothing goes into their brains when they are just relaxing. The fact is that we are sending thoughts into our mind at a rate of about seventy times faster than we can verbalize them orally.

What we put into our mind is vital to our emotional, spiritual, and physical well-being. In an earlier book I recommended several healthy thoughts to put into the mind. Here are some examples:

"There is healing power within me. My body fights to keep me healthy."

"I have as much worth and value as anyone in the world. I don't have to prove it. It's mine simply because I am a human being."

"My life has meaning and purpose. I don't have to know what it is, I just know that it is."

"I have a right to express my feelings and opinions."

"I never lose hope."

"I will do whatever it takes to remain healthy."

"I am a positive person."

"I am a healthy person."

"I am not a victim. I am a participant. I put my own thumbprint on the world."

Why would anyone, of any background, any faith, or

any group be unwilling to put healthy thoughts into his mind? There can be nothing but positive benefits from such an exercise. *The Secret* certainly emphasizes the value of healthy thinking

The Principle of Greater Power

The Secret

Both Christians and the teachers of *The Secret* acknowledge that there is a power greater than we; but what is the source of that power? According to *The Secret,* the universe is the great power, the giver of gifts, the responder to our wishes, and the thing to which we are to align ourselves.

The Sacred

According to Christian teaching, God is the great power. He is the giver of all good gifts and the one who responds to our prayers. We are to align ourselves with Him and His will for our lives.

Whether anyone agrees with our concept of God or not, surely he will acknowledge that one who believes in a power greater than self is better off than one who believes it all ends with us. We need an awareness of something or someone greater than we are. This was one of the principles that helped lead to the success of Alcoholics Anonymous. I think we can all agree on the value of believing in the "greater power" principle.

Because of the value of the teachings of *The Secret* and the areas of difference between them and Christian values, we who want to make application of these principles to our life will be helped with some guardrails for our minds.

4

Guardrails for the Mind

In *The Secret* Lisa Nichols is quoted as saying, "Thank God that there's a time delay, that all of your thoughts don't come true instantly. We'd be in trouble if they did. The element of time delay serves you. It allows you to reassess, to think about what you want, and to make a new choice" (p. 22).

I am not sure who made this observation, but I really believe it is true: Real personal freedom is found in our ability to pause after any stimulus and in that pause make a choice. The pause gives us a chance to make a decision about how we want to respond. That same principle applies here.

What are we to do during that time delay? We are to take advantage of the opportunity to screen our desires through our values by asking: "Is this a good thing for me? Will it harm others?"

Clearly we may fix our minds on things that will not be good for us. William Barclay says, "The human mind will always set itself on something and Paul wished to be quite sure that the Philippians would set their minds on the right things. This is something of the utmost importance, because it is a law of life that, if a man thinks of something often enough, he will come to the stage when he cannot stop thinking about it" (Barclay, p. 79). Since this is true, it becomes tremendously important that we make every effort to focus our mind on the best things.

That is why a discovery I made a few years ago is so important to me. I want to guard my thoughts and turn them in the best direction because I believe they are powerful.

New discoveries have been dramatic in my life. Though I have been a pastor and counselor for more than forty-five years, I keep on discovering truth that has been hidden or ignored in past reading. What caught my attention was a passage in Philippians 4:8. In this verse Paul sounds a lot like the writer of *The Secret.* He tells the small band of believers in the church at Philippi just what they should focus their thoughts on. Interestingly, he does not tell them to think about what they will eat, or wear, or how they will survive in the harsh Roman world. Instead he instructs his readers to think on things that are true, honorable, right, pure, lovely, and of good report. Each of those virtues can be a filter through which we may draw our desires and prayers.

It is such a temptation at the end of the day to review all that has gone wrong, to replay all the hurt, the loss, the fear that we can dredge up. Yet it is during those very times that we should, as the old song says, "fall asleep counting [our] blessings," ending the day on a final positive note with thanksgiving.

Applying *The Secret* to Your Life

Now I want to ask and answer a very important question. "What can you as a Christian do to apply the principles of *The Secret* to your life?" The answer:

"Stop being afraid of principles that are new to you. Test them for yourself to see if they are true." In the following section I will suggest ways to apply all the principles of *The Secret* without compromising any of your religious convictions.

Step one: Get in touch with your own desires, your dreams. I use those terms, "dreams" and "desires," synonymously. They are certainly closely related. Our deepest desires are the things we seek and even crave in our lives. If our deep desires do no damage to our moral codes, they are generally good for us. In some respects they "are" who we are.

I do not believe that desires are to be unqualified, uncontrolled, and unexamined. Make a list of your deepest desires. If it is true, as Socrates said, that the unexamined life is not worth living, it is also true that unexamined desires are not worth dreaming. Be specific and make the list as exhaustive as you can. If you desire a new home, describe the home and the location where you want it. If you want to change jobs, describe the job you want and even list the salary. It doesn't matter how long or short the list is, just that it is your list.

Step two: Next I suggest that you apply a set of guidelines to weed out what is not best for you or what is actually not consistent with your deepest desires. You can do that by examining them in the light of Paul's letter to the Philippians.

Paul's instruction for prayer is a way to examine the principle of thinking, feeling, and asking as set forth in *The Secret.* Before you decide to exercise the magnetic fields of your mind through thought, feeling, and request, it would be good to examine your desires in the light of Philippians 4:8. So go over your list one by one and examine it in light of the following principles.

Are Your Desires True?

One by one look at your desires. The first test here is to check it against your own nature. There are certain things that I know are consistent with me and with what I need to fulfill my life. These include the necessities of life. There are other things that are consistent with my nature too. I want to be open to receiving all the things that are part of who I am.

It is the same principle that I apply to nature. If I were an apple tree, I would pray to produce wonderful apples. I would not pray to produce bad apples. It would not help anyone for me to be reluctant to produce the best and most that I could. The same is true for my human requests. I want to receive and use the things that are best for me.

If you are willing to joyfully receive what is true to your nature, riches, creativity, love, position, or anything else, then receive it and use it for your own joy and for the joy of others.

My list includes writing. I want to write. I believe that writing is consistent with who I am. As long as I can remember, it has been a desire of mine. I am willing to receive this gift in any form that it comes to me. My list does not include becoming a great singer. I enjoy singing, but I have no desire to get the training and practice needed to be a singer. I don't even think my voice is suited for that profession. It would not be true to my nature to ask for great singing ability.

Are your desires consistent with what you are? If your desires are true to your deepest desires, you will be willing to pay the price for what you want. In other words, if you desire an education, and that is your true desire, then not only will you be interested in the end result, an education, but you will also want to participate in the process. You will be willing to pay the price of the hard work involved. If you are not willing to do those things, then your desire does not pass the test of "truth." Now, you may be willing to think about it and even to talk about what you would have to do to pursue an education. You may even imagine yourself receiving the degree. That would feel good, but without the commitment of discipline and hard work, it is not a desire that is true to you.

When you focus on what is true, it will be drawn to you. That is certainly a valid principle, and it brings wonderful results. I discovered this fact years ago when I dreamed of getting a degree from Washington University in St. Louis. I had even drawn a picture of myself in cap and gown receiving that degree, but I had never gone to Washington University. I had finished an undergraduate degree and two master's degrees from good schools, but my dream had not been realized.

Still I kept the thought in my mind. I realized that if I waited much longer, the opportunity would be lost forever. Yet, I did not have the money needed to attend. Though I honestly wanted to enroll, I had no idea if I qualified for graduate study. Still, there was the picture of me in the cap and gown in my mind. Finally I called the university for an interview. As part of the enrollment process I had to pass the Miller Analogy Test with a sufficiently high score for admission.

I sat in my office one day thinking about it. It seemed that the time was right and that if I continued to wait it simply would not happen.

I began to prepare. I met with friends who helped me with Greek mythology, English literature, math, and science. Within six months I was ready for the test. And because I was ready, I passed.

I then applied for admission to the PhD program in counseling psychology only to be told that there was only one opening that year which the admissions committee hoped to fill with a qualified black female. Though I was disappointed, I was not deterred. I asked if I could meet with the admissions committee anyway. They agreed to let me do so. Imagine my delight when I walked out of that meeting as a probationary candidate.

That, however, was not the last hurdle. I needed money for tuition. I sold my only real estate holdings, which happened to be two cemetery plots, and acquired enough money to pay for the first semester. That was the end of my financial resources. But before the end of the first semester, Dr. John Whitely asked me if I would be willing to supervise a small group of master's degree students in counseling. In return the school would cover all my tuition and fees for the next semester. I agreed to do it.

At the end of the second semester, the arrangement got even better. I was offered a similar opportunity for the next two semesters, but this time I received a thousand dollars in addition to my tuition and fees. That arrangement continued throughout my class work.

After three years of class work, fifteen hundred

hours of internship, oral exams, written exams, and seven years of research to complete a dissertation, I donned that cap and gown—the one I had envisioned many years earlier. I received my PhD from Washington University. When you think about a thing, ask for it, and act as if you are going to get it, you generally will. That has been my experience more than once.

One rationale for screening desires through the truth is summed up in the old saying, "Too good to be true." If something sounds too good to be true, it probably is. Proponents of *The Secret* suggest that when we tap into the "secret," things come easily: "You don't have to strain. Nature doesn't strain to produce." The example used is the growing of plants that simply ease up through the earth. Nature certainly doesn't seem to strain, but if we don't exert some effort our desires can run wild. Remember the story about the man who looked out at his friend's field and commented that God had done a beautiful job with the landscape. His friend replied, "Well, you should have seen it when God was doing it all by Himself." Some things appear to be true, but the world is full of illusions and deceptions. It often promises things that it cannot produce, and pursuit of those things can never bring satisfaction. We are wise to examine the thoughts before we dwell on them.

It may be that straining is too strong a word, but make no mistake about it. Most things do not come into our lives without effort and discipline. We may sit in a recliner and hope to learn a foreign language, but until we get up, make application to a school or training program, and begin to work at the process, it's not going to happen.

Losing weight, developing a stronger body, getting an education, overcoming a character flaw, growing spiritually, all of these things come with disciplined effort. If such accomplishments were easy there would be no virtue in their accomplishment. We can't develop good health by wishing.

My oldest son sometimes says to me before we work out at the gym, "Dad, let's go get into shape in one day." We both laugh at the absurdity of this comment. We know that hours, days, and months of hard and continuous work are required to achieve that goal.

What makes a desire true for you is, at the very least, a willingness to pay the price for its achievement. Yes, you can have most any honest desire of your heart, but don't sit on the couch and wait for it to appear. Get up and go for it!

While your thought—your desire—may be the seed that was planted by divine impulse, it can only grow if it is weeded of fear, watered with sweat, and nurtured with action.

Effort is not a bad thing. It may be that you have exerted too little of it in your life. You may have a "something for nothing" desire on some level, but that is not a notion that you should promote. Instead, you should adopt a "can-do" and "will-do" attitude.

Are Your Desires Honorable and Honest?

Paul suggested to the Philippians that they should think on honorable things. Some translate that word as "honest" and others say "worthy." Whatever is worthy of the best in you would be a desirable thing to consider. So ask about each desire, "Is what I deeply desire an honorable thing?"

I knew a married man who said that he had prayed to get out of his marriage and to find a woman who would be better suited for him. He found that woman, "the answer to his prayer," but she was married to another man. Convinced that she was the answer to his prayer, he set out to woo her away from her husband and at the same time set in motion the necessary steps to get a divorce from his own wife. He did succeed in his quest, but I doubt that such a desire is honorable.

It would have been a more honorable desire if his prayer had been that his present wife could become the partner that he desired and that he could be the partner who would be appropriate for her. Thinking positive thoughts about his present relationship and being willing to build on it would be an honorable thing. The only exception would be if he were in an abusive relationship.

If your dream does not measure up to the honorable test, be willing to adjust the dream to something that will be appropriate and will achieve much the same results in your life.

William Barclay adds that the word translated "honorable" is the Greek word *semnos* (Barclay, p. 79). It is hard to translate, but it can be said to mean things that are serious and dignified as opposed to flippant and cheap. Certainly the Christian will want to focus on what is honorable.

There is room in life for flippant moments. But the

deepest desires of our hearts are not cheap and flippant if they are honorable.

A desire is honorable if it is honest. An honest desire is one that is truly wanted. Columbus had an honest desire to prove that the world was round. It was true to his nature, and it was a desire that was so honest he was willing to risk his life for it. That is the ultimate test of honor and honesty for a dream. Most of us will not be that committed to our dreams, but if we were, they would all likely come true. Do you really want the things on your list?

Are Your Desires Just?

Is what you want, deeply want, right for you and for others? If so, it is just. Just things are those things that keep your focus on duty to God and to others. While some people avoid thinking in terms of duty, the Christian's thoughts include it. Ultimate joy and deep satisfaction cannot be achieved if you forget about duty and justice.

The example above concerning desiring someone else's mate would be an illustration of this test, but there are certainly many others. One example that comes to mind is the desire one might have to sell a house and buy another. If the desire to sell does not consider the effect of the sale on the buyer, it is probably not a just desire.

My wife and I consciously made the decision to sell our home to someone who would really enjoy living in it. We asked potential buyers, "Do you think you would enjoy living in this house?"

We also asked for a house that would be right for us,

one that would feel right, and bring joy to us. We found the buyer and the new home. I believe it was a just request.

Striving for something that is inconsistent with basic values cannot be a gift of the universe. Only people without a sense of conscience would be satisfied to go after just anything they desire. I don't want to be absurd, but at that risk I want to point out that none of us would want a pedophile or a serial killer to think on the things he desires. It is careless to proclaim a principle that is intended for rational and basically good people without indicating guidelines.

A part of a just desire is a willingness to pay the price for that desire. If you want a trip around the world, are you willing to learn something about the countries you desire to visit? You can learn of their transportation systems and a few words of their language. That would make your desire more just and the reception of it more fulfilling.

Once when I was in Greece, I decided to attempt to hitch a ride into a village where the locals were planning a bazaar. An auto stopped. There were two young men in it. The one opposite the driver rolled down the window and asked, *"Parlez-vous français?"* I said, "No."

He said, *"Habla español?"* I said, "No."

He sighed, *"Sprechen sie Deutsch?"*

I gave the same answer. He rolled up the window, and they drove away. I vowed then that I would learn enough words to at least get a ride in the countries that I visited in the future. I was not prepared to receive the ride that was provided for me.

Preparation is sending out ships. We cannot justly expect to have our ships come in if we have not sent any out. Asking in that way is irresponsible. We may receive the answer, but it does not pass the test of a just desire. Ultimately I don't see how that can be a good thing.

Limitations are still a part of the fulfilled life. "The love of Christ constrains us" (2 Corinthians 5:14). With this principle accepted, we can generally have anything we really want. My wife and I could have sold our home without concern for the effect on the buyer. That desire could have been fulfilled, simply because we asked for a buyer, but that is not what we wanted. There were limitations on our desire. There are some wants that need to be examined and even restrained. No, that will not go without saying. We are wise to say it again and again.

Are Your Desires Pure?

Is the desire on your list coming from a pure motive, and will it produce pure results? The biblical book of James says that we do not have because we do not ask, but we may ask and not receive because we ask "amiss" (James 4:2). Asking "amiss" is asking with the wrong motive, generally greed or lust. If our motive is pure, and what we want is pure in the sense that it will not harm us or others, we can receive the thing for which we ask. That asking will include time spent thinking about our desire and acting as if we are going to receive it.

"Do I want people in my life simply so that I can use them to achieve my own desires?" "Do I want things that will necessitate hurting others when I obtain them?" These are questions we will ask ourselves if we are concerned about goodness and purity. As Christians, we cannot feel comfortable praying for things and letting the chips fall where they may. That is another limitation on the concept of asking and receiving.

This world is filled with things that are shabby, soiled, and smutty. When we permit ourselves to engage in unrestrained thinking, our mind can become so damaged that it influences all our thoughts. Not every thought that comes into our mind should be permitted to take root there. We need to filter our thoughts and control them.

Are Your Desires Lovely?

Do the things on your list of desires meet the test of loveliness?

The Greek word that is translated "lovely" in Philippians 4:8 is the word *prosphiles* and literally means "that which calls forth love." Thoughts of bitterness and revenge need to be purged and replaced with thoughts of reconciliation and love. Those are attractive thoughts.

Is your desire lovely? Will it be attractive in your life? I believe we are to ask for beauty to fill our lives. I want lovely people in my life. That loveliness is often inside them. I ask for a lovely place to live, lovely clothes, and the ability to see loveliness in everything around me. This is a truth that enriches my life and enriches the lives of people around me. The loveliest thing in the world is probably love itself. We all can freely and confidently ask for someone to love and for someone to love us. This is a request that will bring beauty into our lives.

Are Your Desires of Good Report?

Are your desires of good report? Are they something that can be joyfully shared with others? Of course there is more to "a good report" than what others will think of what you do or how it will affect them. The phrase "of good report" is said by some to mean "high toned" or things that are thought well of. Are your desires something that will be thought well of?

A part of a good report is the way we report what is going on in our life. Some people love to report bad things. When we ask them about their lives, they are quick to tell us that they are miserable, unhappy, not feeling well, and discouraged. *The Secret* is consistent with spiritual truth in emphasizing positive reports. We really can change our lives by making "good reports." We can transform negatives into positives. "I am well and happy. I am optimistic about the future. I live with hope and believe in hope for tomorrow, no matter what is happening today." I am not suggesting that we lie to ourselves and give a phony report of our situation, but we can certainly influence the outcome in our life when we begin to focus on the positive realities. Ask for things in your life that are positive and of good report.

Conclusion of Guardrails

I believe we can apply the principle of attracting things in our life by asking for them, but I also believe that as Christians we should want to ask for things that are true, honest, just, pure, lovely, and of good report. We should think about these things.

A Dramatic Example

Here is an example of what can happen when we apply the best principles of *The Secret* and temper them with the highest values or laws of the spiritual. I can think of no more dramatic example to illustrate the point than Walter Russell.

Walter Russell achieved greatness in varied areas of life. He was an accomplished musician. He was a painter and then a sculptor. (He sculpted the Mark Twain memorial sculpture on display in Hannibal, Missouri. He sculpted the Four Freedoms work that is on display in Hyde Park, New York. He was commissioned to sculpt busts of Franklin D. Roosevelt and Thomas Edison, among others. His work is acclaimed as some of the best ever done.) He was an accomplished architect, designing high-rise buildings in New York City. He was a champion ice skater. Perhaps his greatest accomplishments are still being studied in the area of natural science, especially in relationship to light and balance in the universe. His achievements are well documented and available for study.

Russell's life is chronicled in a powerful little book titled *The Man Who Tapped the Secrets of the Universe,* written by Glenn Clark. In his interviews with this genius, Clark asked him for the secret of his success. Mr. Russell, who never went beyond the eighth grade, gave the following "key" to his success:

"I have absolute faith that anything can come to one

who trusts to the unlimited help of the Universal Intelligence that is within so long as one works within the law and always gives more to others than they expect and does it cheerfully and courteously" (Clark, p. 14).

Note the limitation "so long as one works within the law and always gives more to others than they expect."

There are guidelines to be followed. Walter Russell further explained his own view of those guidelines (which I believe are consistent with the guidelines I have outlined in this chapter). He says there are *five laws* to success for him. They are:

Humility (Until a person learns to lose himself, he cannot find himself);

Reverence (He entered his studio with the recognition that he was a co-creator with the Universal Thinker of all things, God);

Inspiration (He spent time alone and listened to what nature and God were saying to him);

Deep purpose (There is no use for energy of any kind whatsoever unless there is a plan back of it); and,

Joy (The greater the joy an individual finds in achievement, the more energy for moving forward that person has).

We can ask and receive, dream and realize, envision and bring into existence most anything in the world, if we ask, dream, and envision within the guardrails of the mind.

The Possibilities Are Real, But So Are the Guidelines

The point is that Philippians 4:8 gives us a menu of things to put into our mind. These are the kind of things we are to think. When we "think about these things," we will bring them into our life. So, we should think of things that are true, just, pure, lovely, and of good report. Practicing these thoughts will surely bring good things into our life.

We develop habitual thoughts. If we fail to exercise control early in the thought processes, thoughts become habits.

> I am your constant companion. I am your greatest helper or heaviest burden. I will push you onward or drag you down to failure. I am completely at your command. Half the things you do you might just as well turn over to me and I will be able to do them quickly and correctly. I am easily managed. You must merely be firm with me. Show me exactly how you want something done and after a few lessons I will do it automatically. I am the servant of all great men; and alas, of all failures, as well. Those who are great I have made great. Those who are failures I have made failures. I am not a machine, though I work with all the precision of a machine plus the intelligence of a man. You may run me for profit or run me for ruin—it makes no difference to me. Take me, train me, be firm with me, and I will place the world at your feet. Be easy with me and I will destroy you. Who am I? I am habit!
>
> Anonymous (Kimbro, p. 133)

Develop the habit of screening your desires. Be true to the best in you, and ask what you desire.

5

Asking for What We Desire

We Screen Our Desires, Then We Ask for Them

What about "asking" as a principle of attraction in the universe? As indicated earlier, Christians are certainly taught to ask. This is a principle that should bother no one. Jesus said that those who ask will receive, and those who seek will find (Matthew 7:7-8). He assures us that if we know how to give good gifts to those who ask us, the heavenly Father will give good gifts to those who ask Him (v. 11). The Scriptures teach us in the book of James that we do not have because we do not ask (4:2).

We ask with more than our words. We can be creative in our asking by applying some of the principles affirmed in *The Secret*.

We Ask through Thoughts

Thoughts are a form of asking.

It is generally accepted as a biblical concept that "as we think, so are we." Jesus taught that it is not what is on the outside (behavior) that condemns a person, but what is on the inside (thoughts).

In a sense, our thoughts become our dreams, and our dreams shape our lives. This is a principle that has repeatedly expressed itself in my life. It seems safe to say then that one way we ask is through focused thinking about the things we desire.

Glenn Clark wrote a wonderful book expressing this concept. It is called *The Soul's Sincere Desire.* In it he says that what we want and think in the depths of our being is our real prayer.

We Ask through Visualization

Visualizing is another way we ask for things. We see them in our mind and hold them in our mind until they become realities. That includes changes we want to make in our life. When we hold an image in our mind, we are asking for that image to be fulfilled.

We can definitely improve skills, enhance health, and attract things to us though the use of visualization. I doubt that we have even scratched the surface of the power of all the methods suggested in *The Secret,* and this certainly includes visualizing.

In 1967 my life was enriched by Joseph Murphy's book *The Power of Your Subconscious Mind.* Much of what he wrote perfectly coincides with *The Secret.*

He wrote, "What you form in your imagination is as real as any part of your body. The idea and the thought are real and will one day appear in your objective world if you are faithful to your mental image" (p. 78).

Visualization has been used to aid in physical healing, through affecting body physiology in a general way by relaxing the body. That process is called autogenic therapy and uses a series of visualization exercises to facilitate autogenic (brain-directed, self-generating) impulses that assist the human body in the recuperative processes (Luthe).

Schultz and Luthe cite more than 2,400 studies on autogenic therapy. The discoveries in those studies are truly amazing. By the use of imagery (visualizing), researchers have demonstrated a change in muscle potential, blood sugar, white blood cell counts, blood pressure, breathing, heart rate, thyroid secretion, and brain wave patterns. They discovered that they could cause the hypothalamus to moderate the autogenic nervous system and produce healing physiological changes.

In *Seeing with the Mind's Eye,* Samuels and Samuels observe that the use of imagery or visualization in medical treatment has deep roots in history. "Indeed, visualization as a technique to aid in physical healing predates the rise of experimental science. It was probably the most ancient healing technique used by primitive man" (p. 255).

The power and effectiveness of visualization has been repeated, used, and researched in the field of athletics. Investigators have found that visualizing shooting free throws with no actual practice of shooting them is more effective than practice alone.

I have used the technique with consistent success while working with both college and professional athletes. For one example, I taught several pitchers to visualize their pitching motion from the time they received the sign from the catcher until they saw the ball go into the catcher's mitt. Their stories are documented in several articles and personal stories. The pitchers found that their control and confidence were appreciably improved by the use of "visualization tapes."

I have also used the technique with sales training, personal success, weight loss, and most dramatically with cancer patients. I took my lead from Carl and Stephanie Simonton. He is an oncologist, and she is a psychologist. Together they developed a treatment program based, in part, on visualization for cancer patients. Their work is reported in a book, *Getting Well Again*.

One of the most remarkable things they said concerning this process is this: "Relaxation and mental imagery are among the most valuable tools we have found to help patients learn to believe in their ability to recover from cancer. . . . We have discovered that mental imagery is not only an effective motivational tool for recovering health, but is also an important tool for self-discovery in other areas of life" (p. 129).

One cancer patient, with whom I worked, in my seven-year research project at a local research hospital, reported that she became so convinced of the power of visualization in helping her to recover from cancer that she continues to use it in other aspects of her life. She was told that the radiation she had received had so damaged her vocal cords that she would never be able to sing again. She visualized healthy vocal cords and saw herself singing for weddings. She said, "I visualize my body fighting all infections. My hair is growing back, and my singing voice is about 60 percent back. I wish my father could have known about these methods. He died of cancer two years ago. I really feel strengthened by this program. I am a Muhammed Ali [prizefighter] in my fight against cancer. I am not afraid."

She has been cancer free for twenty years, and she sings at weddings.

I have seen the results of concentrated visualization repeatedly. I know it works.

I first became aware of this technique in the mid-1970s. I read Carl and Stephanie Simonton's book *Getting Well Again.* In the book they wrote of the use of visualization to help cancer patients engage the power of their own immune systems to fight malignancies. I saw it effectively help many cancer patients in our work in St. Louis.

I also have seen it work with baseball players, basketball players, golfers, weightlifters, and other athletes. By practicing visualization, baseball pitchers have learned to control their pitches better than they ever thought possible.

One Fortune 500 company asked me to make a visualization tape for their salespeople. I did, and as far as I know they are still using it to help salespeople prepare for sales calls.

I believe that the ability to imagine or visualize is a God-given gift, and I use it regularly. I not only picture things that I want to achieve, but I talk to myself about those things. I give myself positive input all the time. Jesus Christ said that it is not the things outside us that defile us, but the things inside us (Matthew 15:18-20). It is also the things that we put inside us through our thought processes and imagery that make us strong and successful.

We Ask with Gratitude

This principle rightly follows a discussion concerning desires. When we receive the things we request, it is not only logical but powerful for us to give thanks.

One of the most impressive sections of the *The Secret* is the discussion of gratitude. Once we have processed our thoughts and dreams through the filters of value, we are free to ask for what we want, but we are to do it with a spirit of gratitude. In the passage in Philippians 4, Paul says that requests should be made to God with gratitude. We are to express thanksgiving in all things.

The practice of gratitude makes us capable of receiving the things we desire. None of us can lift ourselves by our own shoelaces; we all need and depend on others. Some of us recognize that we also depend on God. That recognition puts us in a constant state of gratitude.

We all need reminders. My own practice is to begin giving thanks first thing in the morning. Before my feet hit the floor I thank God for another day of life.

One of the laws of thanksgiving is that we are to give thanks not only for what we have received, but also for the things we are going to receive. If we ask for something, and we are trusting that we will receive it, we can immediately give thanks for it.

The attitude of gratitude is the opposite of the spirit of complaining. Gerald Mann tells a wonderful story about his family. They had lost everything in a flood in Texas. They were standing in floodwaters when his father started laughing. His mother could not understand how he could laugh at such a time. Mr. Mann said that they had lost things and that they could replace things, then he added, "I am gladder that we had all those things than madder that we lost them." That is a spirit of gratitude.

Lost a marriage? Mad about it? Were there good

times? Were their children? Can you be gladder that you had the relationship than madder that you lost it? Give thanks for what you had. It makes you more receptive to a new relationship.

Nothing prepares us for gifts and achievements in life like a grateful spirit. "In everything by prayer and supplication, *with thanksgiving,* let your requests be made known to God" (Philippians 4:6, emphasis added).

The only question I have about the focus on gratitude in *The Secret* concerns motive. "Gratitude is a powerful process for shifting your energy and bringing more of what you want into your life. Be grateful for what you already have, and you will attract more good things" (p. 93). As Christians we are admonished to give thanks in everything, not in order to get more things, but simply to express an honest gratitude to God for all of His grace and gifts in our life.

We Ask through Focus

The Secret says, "Instead of focusing on the world's problems, give your attention and energy to trust, love, abundance, education, and peace" (p. 153). Surely no one will have any problem accepting and applying this principle.

The skill of focus is the skill necessary for developing and maintaining a positive outlook on life. Few people would contradict the notion that a positive outlook is essential for living an effective life. We determine the focus in our own life. We cannot control the things that happen to us, but we can choose how we will view them.

This process of changing focus is called by many of us "reframing." We frame the pictures in our own lives. We put our own spin on the experiences that come our way.

Some Points on Focusing on the Positive

1. Positive focus puts attention, not on the event or circumstance, but on the results of the event. If I were a salesperson, a client may have rejected me. For me that is not a positive thing. However, the result can be positive, if I learn from the experience. I can grow stronger through most of my difficult experiences.

I learn as I think back over my presentation and think of things I might have said or that I may have missed in the communication. If I learn one thing, the experience has been positive.

I grow stronger because I am able to see that the rejection is not devastating. In fact, I can handle it. My youngest son has for years been in sales. He got an interview with a large pharmaceutical company and was ultimately turned down. I called him and asked if he was doing all right. He responded, "I'm fine, Dad. I'm a salesman. I'm used to rejection. It happens every day. If you can't handle a little rejection, you can't make it in sales. You just go on believing the next time you will make the sale."

I would add that if you can't handle a little rejection, you may not make it in life. We all are going to experience some rejection. Even Jesus Christ was rejected by His own people (John 1:11). If you grow a little in your ability to handle rejection as a result of an apparent failure in sales, you have a positive result.

2. Positive focus means just that—focusing on the positive, not the negative. I look for something positive in whatever happens. I am not dumb enough or unrealistic enough to think that everything that happens is good. There are some rotten things that happen to all of us. It is almost psychotic to think that everything is good.

I'm talking about the person who falls flat on his backside on the ice and says, "Wow, that was a wonderful experience." That is not being honest. But he could even make it a religious fall by saying something like, "Praise the Lord, I just fell flat on my behind. I'm really glad for the experience."

Falling is not, for me, a wonderful experience, but I try to find something positive in it. An example would be, "I'm glad I didn't break my arm or leg. Maybe this little spill will make me more careful." Now I have a positive result.

The truth is that there is usually something positive, even in the worst experiences of life. Our problem is that we are not geared up to look for the positive. We compound the tragedies of life by not learning and growing as a result of them.

Keep your mind on the positives of life. As Earl Nightingale says, "The secret of happiness is keeping your mind on the things you want and off the things you don't want."

3. Ask questions that will help you focus your mind on the positive. When something bad happens ask, "What is good about this situation?" If you practice the right questions, you will find more of the positive things in life. No matter what happens, learn to ask,

"What is positive here? What can I learn from this experience?" If you ask better questions you will get better answers.

4. You will generally find what you are looking for. If you look long enough for a negative consequence, you will find it. Conversely, if you look consistently for a positive consequence, you will find that too.

For years, my mother, whom I call the champion worrier of the world, warned me that I might have an accident. She told me that before every trip I made for years. I drove for more than five hundred thousand miles all across this nation and never even had a bent fender. Then one night while driving home in East Texas the car I was driving was hit by an auto driven by a drunken man. No one was seriously injured, but when I called my mother and told her about it she gave me this response: "I told you so." That incident was enough to confirm her negative predictions of fifteen years

It doesn't take many negative events to convince the average negative thinker that he is right. Some suggest that it takes about two dozen positive statements to offset one negative. This is true because we have all been given so much negative input in our lives that one statement can trigger the years of training. Even in taking tests we often focus on the negative, noting how many answers we got wrong rather than how many we got right.

If I am likely to find the things I am looking for, I am going to look for the positives. If I look first for positives, I am much more likely to find them. Again, I do not want to be unrealistic, but I do want to give myself a chance to see the positives in everything possible.

To paraphrase an old song, "Accentuate the positive, and reduce the impact of the negative."

We are all given twenty-four hours each day. We choose the way we use those hours. We choose how long we work, rest, worry, exercise, eat, pray, play, or watch television. All the activities of life fall under the heading of personal choices, and yet we are not trained in conscious decision making. The skill of choosing is often unrefined and unconscious. Give some serious thought to this vital skill and work to make it part of your life.

It begins with the awareness that you have choices.

It is done most effectively by gathering information.

It concludes with the courage to choose.

We Focus through Awareness

Many people go through life without the slightest notion that they are making decisions every day. Many think that life is just happening to them. Begin your new focus on the positive with a dramatic awareness.

6
Major Issues for Christians in *The Secret*

There is a secret that was missed in most of *The Secret.* That is the secret of balance and contentment. Paul wrote about it later in the fourth chapter of Philippians. He said that he had learned *the secret* of being content, no matter what his outward circumstances. He said that he could be content with a lot or with a little because he could do all things through Christ who gave him strength (Philippians 4:7-13 NIV).

Christian philosophy is optimistic and positive and is still able to remain rooted in truth. The truth is that even the most beautiful lives and the most right-thinking people still face difficulties. Jesus Christ was the most gentle, the most positive, the kindest, most loving person who ever lived. He certainly tapped into the power of healing and abundance. Yet He was betrayed, rejected, beaten, and crucified.

There are a number of other examples of positive people who suffered adversity both in Bible times and in our day. They include people like Joseph, David, Paul, Mahatma Gandhi, Nelson Mandela, and Martin Luther King, Jr. This suggests that even the most positive thinkers experience some negative things. Any complete and honest approach to life must include this awareness and add coping lessons along with the other principles they teach. It is clear that Christian teaching does that and thus maintains a balance that is necessary for truth.

Merit Versus Grace

One major issue we must deal with is the idea that we deserve all the good things we can get. In Christian thinking deserving has little to do with what we receive. Grace has a lot to do with it.

When I view the suffering of so many people I have a hope for more generosity and less greed in the world in which we already have enough to go around. One of the problems is that people who already have enough to live comfortably for the rest of their lives want more and try to hoard what they already have. Jesus warned against this kind of selfishness in the Sermon on the Mount. He said that we are to lay up treasures in heaven and not on earth, warning, "For where your treasure is, there your heart will be also" (Luke 12:34). This principle is not emphasized by teachers of *The Secret.* They apparently believe what Henry Ford said when he was asked how much money was enough: "One dollar more than you have."

Here is another great secret. Deserving has little to do with anything. Grace and mercy have a lot to do with life. I don't know what people deserve. I just know that it doesn't matter what they deserve; the reality is that some have a lot, and others have a little.

We might think that Jesus would have been better off if He had been more loving, virtuous, focused on healing and helping, trusting, and faithful . . . but wait a minute. He was all of those things, and still He was rejected and crucified. There are some things that are simply going to happen, even to the very best people.

I don't know why bad things happen to good people who focus on love and grace. In some instances genetics play a role. Other problems result from the failure of others around us. It may be in part our failures, but I guarantee you that not everything that happens to us is a result of our attracting it into our life; some of it, perhaps, but not all of it.

A lovely young woman went to a party one night. Her sister drove to the party to pick her up. Both girls and their parents were devoted Christians. On the way home that night, an intoxicated driver sped through a red light and struck their car, instantly killing the younger girl. I walked with that family through the pain and distress. They never lost their positive focus and faith. I marveled at them. It is nearly repulsive for me to think that any of them "attracted" that event to themselves. I continued to urge them to hold visions of love and grace. They did.

Who would be so callous as to suggest that rape victims attracted their rapists? That is tantamount to agreeing with the harsh evaluation, "They were asking for it." A child playing on a schoolground is not attracting a pedophile. That child is not thinking fearful thoughts of assault. I believe the statement in *The Secret* that "nothing can come into your experience unless you summon it through persistent thoughts" (p. 43) goes a step too far.

I have dealt with the fine line between responsibility and blame through all the years of my work with cancer patients. I try to be realistic with them. There are certainly some situations in which the patient, through denial or ignorance, has contributed to the onset of cancer. This is true of some of those who have smoked or have followed other poor health habits. At the same time those people did not intend to get cancer, and some were just genetically predisposed to it. Others were the victims of environmental conditions that were "not of their own making." *There simply must be balance and restraint in presenting helpful principles.* This surely applies to the "law" of attraction.

Every Philosophy and Religion Advances through Evangelism

One of the great principles of any effective movement is that in order for it to continue, there must be a way to share it. This is done through written materials, television and radio, videos, cassette tapes, DVDs, and personal testimonies. Those who spread *The Secret* use all of these methods. Their leaders are prophets, doctors, visionaries, philosophers, writers, and therapists. Some of them are surely as much zealots as are some of the fundamentalist Christian preachers.

Christianity is dependent on the same vehicles of communication. We believers have our written materials, radio and television programs, videos, cassettes, DVDs, and individual witnesses. Our leaders are clergy persons, religious teachers, and dedicated lay people.

Both *The Secret* and The Sacred have their adherents and their evangelists. We all attempt to share good news. Dr. Denis Waitley catches that truth in his comment: "Most of the leaders in the past missed the great part of The Secret, which is to empower and share with others" (p. 152). That is what we are all to do with the knowledge that we have.

The Reasons for Failure

Even in the best of circumstances things don't always work out the way they are planned. When failures occur, we begin to look for reasons. It is hard for us to acknowledge that we just don't know enough to answer all the questions of life, so we look for someone or some thing on which to place blame or responsibility. *The Secret* teaches that when we fail to get what we want, it is clearly our fault: "You didn't really believe, or you stopped too soon" (*The Secret,* DVD).

Robert Collier is quoted on this topic in *The Secret.* He says, "If you have any lack, if you are prey to poverty or disease, it is because you do not believe or do not understand the power that is yours" (p. 150).

Again, it is stated that "the only reason any person does not have enough money is because they are *blocking* money from coming to them with their thoughts" (p. 99). The basic philosophy and teaching of *The Secret* seems to be: "Whatever negative thing happens to you, it is your fault."

Christians sometimes use the same rationalization. "I'm sure God would have given me what I asked if I had just had enough faith." Jesus did say, "According to your faith will it be done to you" (Matthew 9:29 NIV). People whose prayers for healing are not answered are often told that they simply didn't have enough faith. That is not what Christian Scriptures teach. The apostle Paul prayed for his "thorn in the flesh" (2 Corinthians 12:7) to be removed. It never was. He was told by God that it didn't matter, because His grace would be sufficient for him (vv. 8-10). Not all prayers will be answered, and not all wishes will be fulfilled, but that is no reason to stop praying or stop wishing.

Even those who claim to have great faith often falter in the difficult times. My grandmother told me about a woman who believed that Jesus literally meant that if we have faith we can say to a mountain, "Be removed and be cast into the sea" and "it will be done" (Matthew 21:21). She said that the woman stood before a mountain, closed her eyes, and prayed for the mountain to be removed. She then opened her eyes and said, "Just as I expected. It is still here." That probably describes the faith of a lot of people. Still, I agree with the idea that God will do, in answer to the prayer of the weakest, most doubting one of us, what He could not otherwise get done. I identify with the man who said, "Lord, I believe; help my unbelief!" (Mark 9:24).

I do not believe we can always blame the person who is praying for failure to receive. There are just too many dynamics that are beyond our ability to know or understand. We must simply keep on praying and keep on expecting all the wonderful things that we can.

One of the teachers of *The Secret* suggests that if we have trouble believing in the big things, we should start with something small, like asking for a cup of coffee. I agree that we can begin with "faith-sized requests" and build our faith from that point, but we must remember that faith continues to seek, even after disappointments.

Two Fundamental Problems with *The Secret*

Depending on Law

The use of the word "law" in *The Secret* is apparently intended to build faith in the concepts taught in this material. For example, the law of attraction is said to be as consistent as the law of gravity. After referring to the law of gravity this statement follows, "The law of attraction is a law of nature. It is as impartial and impersonal as the law of gravity is" (p. 27).

There are surely some exceptions to the "law of attraction." Reference has already been made to what seem to be obvious exceptions. These include many diseases, rape, murder, death from a suicide bomber, or suffering in a concentration camp. There are many other examples. It seems to detract from the powerful reality that we influence much of what we are and what comes into our lives by overstating the truth. For me the lessons are more honest and still powerful if we speak in terms of the *principle* of attraction, not the *law* of attraction.

Deifying the Universe

It is certainly troublesome for Christians that in *The Secret,* the word "universe" is deified and consistently capitalized ("Universe") in the same way that Christians would capitalize "God" or "Jesus."

Most Christians have a major problem referring to the universe as God, but it is clear that this is exactly what happens in *The Secret.* Some of the more obvious examples of deifying the universe may be seen in the following comparisons.

1. Christians are taught to ask in order to receive. The clear implication of the teaching of Jesus is that we are to ask God, who will answer our prayers.

In *The Secret* the teachers claim they are applying a lesson from the New Testament by instructing readers to make their desires known to the universe, as Lisa Nichols states. "The first step is to ask. Make a command to the Universe. Let the Universe know what you want. The Universe responds to your thoughts" (p. 47).

2. Christians are taught to trust in God. The apostle Paul wrote that "we should not trust in ourselves but in God who raises the dead" (2 Corinthians 1:9).

In *The Secret* readers are taught to trust in the universe. "Trust the Universe. Trust and believe and have faith" (p. 57).

3. Christians are taught that they should turn themselves over to God and trust Him to provide for them.

In *The Secret* readers are told to turn themselves over to the universe. Dr. Joe Vitale says, "If you turn it [your life] over to the Universe, you will be surprised and dazzled by what is delivered to you. This is where magic and miracles happen" (p. 85).

Some may argue that it doesn't really matter what we call God. That is hard for some of us to accept in light of our faith that God created the universe. We look to the Creator rather than to the creation. In Romans 1, after explaining that God was revealed to humanity through creation, Paul writes in verse 21, "For even though they knew God, they did not honor Him as God or give thanks, but they became futile in their speculations."

I read the materials and try to understand them in

light of my own faith. Frequently I simply substitute the word "God" for the word "Universe" in the material. I want to accept and apply truth wherever I find it, but I also want to remain true to my own faith at the same time.

While I have some reticence about jumping on board much of what is generally categorized as "New Age" material, I find a lot of helpful material in many different books and articles that are not necessarily Christian in nature or message. *The Secret* is no exception.

At the same time, it remains a puzzle to me that such a large number of people are willing to embrace faith in an inanimate and invisible universe while rejecting as unintelligent the acceptance of a personal, invisible God. Some seem willing to believe in a mechanical universe, pray to it, thank it, trust in it, and at the same time have trouble trusting in the God of the universe, revealed by Jesus Christ. As my children might say, "Go figure!"

Having said all that, let me reemphasize that there is great value in learning and applying the general principles taught in *The Secret.*

7

Listening to One Another

A curious event changed my perspective. I was serving as pastor of a small church in Northeast Texas. One Sunday evening I approached a small group in a Bible study. I heard what seemed to be an argument going on. As I drew closer I heard one man's voice literally roar out, "I don't care what the science books say. The Bible says that an angel stood on each of the four corners of the earth, and a ball does not have corners. I believe the earth is flat."

I stopped in my tracks and decided that a retreat was the best option, but I did not make it. One of the group members said, "What do you think about that, Pastor?"

I decided to keep moving, but I replied over my shoulder, "That's what the Bible says all right." It did not seem prudent to me to get into that debate.

That is a true story from the late 1950s. Since then I have confronted the same mentality among too many Christians. I wonder why it is so difficult for us to accept truth from sources other than religious documents. That makes no sense to me at all.

Why We Don't Listen

1. We don't listen because we think we already know it all.

It occurs to me that we Christians ought to maintain enough humility to admit that we don't have a monopoly on truth and that we need to be willing to listen to what science, education, medicine, philosophy, and other disciplines have to say. Failure to do so will throw us back into a Dark Ages mentality.

Theologians would be wise to allow scientists to speak to scientific issues, anthropologists to explain the development of humanity, psychologists to describe the nature of human emotions and mental processes, medical people to lead out in health issues, and philosophers to contribute to our understanding of theories of knowledge. It might be that if we listen to them, some of them might listen to us about spiritual issues.

It is dangerous to reject ideas without patiently examining them. St. Augustine said to theologians centuries ago, "In matters that are so obscure and far beyond our vision, we find in Holy Scripture passages which can be interpreted in very different ways without prejudice to the faith we have received. In such cases, we should not rush in headlong and so firmly take our stand on one side that, if further progress in the search for truth justly undermines this position, we too fall with it" (Collins, p. 83).

I point out this truth in order to make a point about the Christian attitude toward the teachings found in *The Secret.* There are many wonderful truths to be embraced in the ideas expressed in it, if correctly interpreted and carefully applied.

As Christians, following the teachings of Jesus, we are to follow the principle of open-mindedness. When people are attempting to contribute to the betterment of humanity, for whatever reason and from whatever background, we would be well advised to listen to what they have to say. We might learn something!

2. We don't listen because ideas come from people who are different from us.

When the disciples of Jesus told Him that they had heard someone practicing faith who was not of their small group, they stopped him. Jesus told the disciples not to stop such people because "who[ever] is not against us is on our side" (Luke 9:50). We need to remember that God has other sheep that are not of our "flock" (John 10:16). Unfortunately, many Christians do not want to hear that message. They somehow believe that we believers have a monopoly on all truth. We don't. We don't even have a monopoly on all religious truth. There is so very much that we do not know.

I love to read things like *The Secret.* I find in such material much that affirms my own faith and much that deepens my understanding of how the mind works. I thank God for the people who spend so much of their lives seeking to uncover truth. More power to them!

One of the things that distresses me more than meeting people outside the religious community who believe that Christians have nothing to offer them is to be aware of Christians who do not believe that anyone outside our faith community has anything helpful to contribute to us.

The result of that kind of closed-mindedness is failure to advance scientific truth among our own young people and to cut ourselves off from valuable information that is readily available to anyone who does not already know everything.

I encouraged all the cancer patients with whom I worked to avail themselves of the power of visualization, the power of goal setting, the power of the mind, and all the knowledge they could find from people who were looking for answers about cancer. I did not care whether the people who discovered those helpful ideas were Christians or not. I just wanted to embrace truth wherever I could find it and channel it to the people who might benefit most from it.

3. We don't listen because we are afraid we will have to give up too many of our own beliefs.

A tolerant approach to the contributions of others does not mean that we are to set aside our diligence in examining those contributions. Nor does it mean that we are under any obligation to embrace all of them. It does mean that we are to keep our mind open and not reject wholesale approaches that we don't understand. We are to examine them and apply the ones that seem helpful to us.

4. We don't listen because we are too lazy to examine new ideas or just too lazy to listen.

A farmer in Kansas is said to have been approached by a representative of the department of agriculture in that state. The rep wanted to teach the farmer some new and improved ways of farming.

The farmer reportedly responded by saying, "I don't want to learn any new ways of doing things."

"Don't you want to learn to farm better?" the representative wondered aloud.

The farmer said, "I already know better than I am doing, so why would I want to learn anything else?"

Examining and applying new ideas requires effort. Most of us have established some pretty lazy listening habits.

I recently drove through a drive-in restaurant. I was asked to give my order at the speaker. I said, "I would like a small strawberry shake."

The response came back, "I'm sorry, we only have one size shake."

"What size do you have?"

The answer was, "We only have small shakes."

I shook my head and said, "I'll take that." We really fail to listen to one another.

One other example gets to this point. A woman in a counseling session was exasperated with her husband's failure to listen. She said that he was so lazy that he not only failed to listen to her, he didn't even listen to himself.

It is sad that we miss so many insights from others because we lack the humility to learn from them, think we already know it all, won't accept information from people who differ from us, fear losing our own beliefs, or are just too lazy to think about anything new.

There are many other reasons or excuses that we may have for not listening to others. Men sometimes refuse to listen to women and vise versa. A small girl summed it up when she said, "Even boys have something to say if you listen long enough."

Racial, political, religious, or ethnic bias keeps us from listening to one another. Some white people will not listen to an African-American. Such arrogance, if practiced by all, would have kept us from learning from George Washington Carver. The nation's farmers would have been impoverished by that failure. The same prejudice would have kept many from hearing the compassionate message of Martin Luther King, Jr. Such failure would have set us back fifty years in the advance toward racial equality.

As ridiculous as it may seem, young people often refuse to listen to an old person, and old people sometimes fail to listen to young people. Mind you, it is not because either is wrong or has nothing to contribute, but simply because one is old and the other is young. This world is certainly justified by its own wisdom (Matthew 11:19 KJV).

5. *We fail to listen because of preconceived ideas.*

We often see and hear what we expect to see and hear, no matter what is real. I spoke to a group of college students a few years ago. I was speaking about depression. At the intermission of the meeting a young woman came up to me and said, "Why do you use only women as illustrations of depression?"

I responded that I had used both men and women as examples. She was positive that I was mistaken. Fortunately, for me, the session was recorded. I asked the young woman to listen to a portion of the presentation with me. Sure enough, there were examples of both men and women used in my talk. She was astounded that she had missed those examples.

I hypothesized that she failed to hear them because she did not expect to hear them.

It was for that very reason that for many years I taped my marriage counseling sessions. On numerous occasions I had to play back a portion of the session to one or the other of the clients because of their failure to listen. Usually it was because something was said that was not expected.

Our preconceived notions can block out reality and truth. We may miss a valuable truth simply because it does not fit with what we think to be the truth. We need to learn to accept the unexpected.

One night my brother, our dad, and I were at a ball game in St. Louis. When we left the stadium, we came to an intersection that was blocked for as far as we could see in front, from both sides, and from the rear.

My brother impatiently and emphatically remarked, "I don't believe this."

My dad, who never missed an opportunity to zing either of us, said, "Well, I wouldn't have expected it, but I can believe it because I see it."

In his humor he had expressed a truth that should be incorporated by all of us. No matter what we expect as a result of our biases, we can believe what we see, if we examine it closely.

6. We fail to listen because listening might mean that we have to change.

I am slow to accept change, slow but not dead. Life means change. Learning means change. Growth means change. The only people who frighten me more than those who want to change everything are the people who do not want to change anything. Failure to change can cause death.

I heard of a farm family that had a large rock that they used for a doorstop. When ask why they used the rock in that way, the answer was, "Pappy stopped plowing one day and sat on that rock in the field. He died on that rock. It was the last rock Pappy ever sat on."

The story goes that one of the family members, after a late night of partying, came through the door, tripped over the last rock that Pappy ever sat on, fell, and broke his neck.

We are not wise to hang on to things just because Pappy believed them, or because our church taught us to believe them, or because some politician said them. We are to accept and make use of things because they are true and helpful. And to do that, we have to listen.

Rejecting new ideas because we have never "done it that way" or because "Pappy never sat on that rock" is a sure way to stunt our emotional and mental growth.

Learn to Listen; Listen to Learn

Whatever the reasons, we often fail to listen. This fact caused one writer to observe, "Communication in America is a competitive exercise between two people, in which the first person to take a breath is declared the 'listener.'" Such observations are not funny when we realize how tragic failure to listen can be.

When I say we are to listen, I mean we are to listen with the intent to hear and apply what we hear when it is appropriate. We haven't really listened until we have acted on what we have heard, either by reasonably rejecting it or by accepting and acting as if we have heard.

I read what is written in *The Secret* and make application of the truths in it that seem to me to be appropriate. I suggest that you do the same.

Learn to listen. It doesn't cost anything to listen, but it may cost you a great deal to fail to listen.

8

How Dreams Are Fulfilled

Does the universe respond to our thoughts and visions by fulfilling our spoken and unspoken requests? That is the explanation that is given in *The Secret.*

On the other hand, Christians believe that, in His infinite grace, God provides the fulfillment of many of our dreams.

I prefer the second explanation, but either approach leaves many questions unanswered. Why are not all of our dreams fulfilled? Why are dreams fulfilled for some people and not for others? I cannot answer those questions, but I know that there is a connection between our deepest desires and the fulfillment we experience in our lives. Let me offer a few examples.

Radio Programs

I had the privilege of doing radio programs on a powerful radio station. I did those programs for more than seventeen years. Looking back I wonder if there is not a way to connect the dots between that experience and early desires in my life.

From the time I was a junior high school student in Southeast Missouri I dreamed of being on the radio. I entertained my siblings in cotton fields by broadcasting baseball games from the introduction of the game to the final out and the sign-off. I learned the names, batting averages, backgrounds, pitching records, and hometowns of most of the players on the St. Louis Cardinal baseball team and a few on the Brooklyn Dodgers. I even did the commercials. It was a ritual that helped us pass the time while working in the fields. I never consciously aspired to be a baseball announcer, but the radio intrigued me. My first real experience of broadcasting was a taped show on humor that I did for the speech department of my college in Marshall, Texas.

I did a few programs, preaching in studio for some small-town churches. I loved listening to the clergy round table discussions on KMOX in St. Louis, Missouri. I often thought it would be fun to do that program. I never did.

I did, however, get called to do a program on marriage and family when I was teaching the course by that name at the social work school at Washington University in St. Louis. The hostess, Ann Keefe, asked me what I thought would be a good format for a program on marriage and family life. I suggested a live counseling program.

I was asked to do some pilot shows in the afternoon and was hired to do a daily program on which I did live counseling. After a few months I had enjoyed about as much of that as I could stand so I asked to reduce the schedule. I went from afternoons to evenings in which I did a program with regular host, Jim White, for seventeen years.

It never seemed like a big thing, but in retrospect, it was an unlikely occurrence. Still, I wonder if I attracted it to myself when I was in the cotton fields. For most Christians, the answer would be that God grants us opportunities, but it is possible that God permits us to use the principles that guide things to us through attraction.

My Wife's Experience

I asked my wife if there was any experience in her life that might affirm the notion that there is a connection between dreams or goals and fulfillment. She reminded me of the following experience.

When we started shutting down the operation of the cancer center, Teresa Gay started thinking about a new job. She decided to write out a description of the job she wanted. She even included the salary that she expected to be paid.

It was only a matter of weeks until she got the exact job that she had described and at the exact salary she had written. I wonder if she attracted that job and salary through her specific goal description.

Experiences Beyond Coincidence

What is the explanation? Surely such experiences are beyond coincidence. My youngest daughter reminds me that for people of faith there is no such thing as coincidence. What appear to be coincidences, she says, are really "God events." Others will explain it as the fulfillment of the law of attraction.

Most of us have had the experience of thinking about people that we haven't heard from in years only to have them call us. "I was just thinking about you," we exclaim in wonder. How many times have you said that? How do we explain that kind of "coincidence"? It could be that there is something to the laws of attraction and focus. Maybe God does work that way.

Just after I finished writing my first book, I met a man who wanted me to speak to a group from his company. I mentioned to him the manuscript I had just finished. He said, "I know an editor who is looking for a self-help book. She says that her company wants to expand its base into that area."

I asked for the name of the editor, called her, she asked to see the manuscript, and within a couple of months we were working out the details for publication.

How can we explain the meeting of the right person at the right time? I often explain it as the answer to prayer. I do pray for right people to come into my life. At the same time, it is possible that the dynamics of situations like that may be influenced by thoughts that we send out. I see no reason for not leaving room for such things in a universe that is as complex and yet as connected as ours is.

As I have said, I believe there is a great deal of truth in the teachings of *The Secret.* I just think that we have to balance that truth with the guardrails for the mind described in chapter 4.

9

What Is Your Wish?

If you knew that your wishes would come true, what would you wish for? If you really had the power to attract results to yourself, what results would you want to attract? Tell me your dreams, and I will tell you your values.

We often lie to ourselves about the things we value. I frequently ask seminar participants to list the five things they value most and to list them in the order of their importance. The usual list, beginning with the most important, is God, family, health, education, and financial security.

When I follow up by asking them to note how much time and energy they devote to each of those "values," the results are almost always the same. Most time and energy are spent on securing money for financial security. Plans are in place for that purpose. The amount of time and energy spirals downward from there, usually in this order: education, family, health, and God. The truth is the opposite of stated values.

Assume for a moment that the law of attraction fully works. What do you want to attract to your life? What do you want for your children? What do you want to attract to your world? How will you go about attracting the things you want into your life? Will you draw pictures of them? Will you focus your thoughts on them?

Will you act as if they are in your life and enjoy the feeling of having them? These are the suggestions of *The Secret.*

My Dreams and Goals

Suppose I have just rubbed the magic lamp, and the genie, the power of the universe, has popped out and said, "Ask what you will, and it will be done. You have no limit to your wishes." I picture myself in that situation. Then, at the risk of turning a stomach or two of those who think I am trying to be overly altruistic, I make my wishes. I know what my priority wishes are. I wish for the fulfillment of my dreams and goals.

Some of my dreams and goals I have already stated. On a personal level, I desire success in writing and continued health for me and for my family. I have plenty of self-satisfying goals. I also have some deeper desires.

My deeper goals and dreams are probably shared by many others, including you. I dream of a world in which nations live at peace and work together to resolve the problems of injustice expressed in poverty and hunger. I dream of a world in which those who have abundance provide for those who have nothing. In other words, I dream of a world in which the kingdom of God comes and His will is done on earth as it is in heaven (Matthew 6:10).

When I try to get specific on the "how-to" of that dream I become hazy. I do believe that we have in place the organization that could potentially be the vehicle for achieving that goal. The United Nations could certainly make strides in that direction if we can ever rise above the enforcement of sanctions and get to a focus on resolving problems.

It would be wonderful if all the people who are dreaming of personal security—cars, homes, and money—would focus their dreams on making the world better for everyone. We all want personal security, but surely we can also have higher desires. I would love security for the rest of my life, but life is short, so I would risk all of it for a world of peace and harmony. I honestly believe that Jesus Christ was right in challenging us to risk everything to follow Him.

What Do You Really Want?

Jesus once called on a rich young man who wanted to find eternal life to sell all that he had, give it to the poor, and then follow Him. The young man went away with sorrow (Matthew 15:19-22). Do you know of anything that you value enough to sacrifice your material possessions to obtain? Is there anything in your life you would consider "the pearl of great price" (Matthew 13:45-46)?

Before you decide to try to get everything you want, you might be wise to work on your "wanter." That truth applies to all of us.

10

The Greatest of These!

The Secret has a lot to say about one of my favorite topics: love. "All your joy is on the frequency of love." It notes that while we can't hold love in our hands, we can feel it in our heart. It says that our ability to love is unlimited, and that when we love we are in harmony with the universe. It urges us to love everyone and everything. "Focus only on things you love . . . and you will experience that love and joy coming back to you—multiplied!" (p. 122).

There is a law of love that we often miss: If you don't love yourself, you are not equipped to love others. It is stated this way in *The Secret:* "To transmit the highest frequency of love, you must love yourself" (p. 172). In the great song of love in the New Testament, found in 1 Corinthians 13, Paul lists three virtues. They are faith, hope, and love. He says that the greatest of these is love (v. 13).

Jesus made the standard for loving others the love of self. "You shall love your neighbor as yourself" (Matthew 19:19). Love is so important that Jesus said loving God and loving your neighbor as you love yourself is the sum total of all religious law (Matthew 22:37-40).

I value this topic so much that I am adding some of my thoughts on love.

What Is Love?

What is love anyway? When that question was posed to a group of children they gave the following responses:

"Love is when a girl puts on perfume and a boy puts on shaving cologne and they go out and smell each other."

"Love is when you go out to eat and give somebody most of your French fries without making them give you any of theirs."

"Love is when you tell a guy you like his shirt, then he wears it every day."

"I know my older sister loves me because she gives me all her old clothes and has to go out and buy new ones."

"When you love somebody, your eyelashes go up and down and little stars come out of you."

We all have our ideas about love. It is at least a positive feeling. Some dictionary definitions of the verb "love" include, "to hold dear," "to cherish," "to like," and "to take pleasure in."

For me, love means acceptance and encouragement. It means a desire for good for the person loved.

We are fortunate if we know that we are loved. Life is difficult. To live without an awareness of being loved can be devastating. But if we know that we are loved we can face just about anything life brings to us.

Self-Love Is Basic

Bernie Siegel says that "the fundamental problem most patients face is an inability to love themselves, being unloved by others during some crucial part of their lives" (Siegel, p. 4). He further observes that "the extent to which we love ourselves determines whether we eat right, get enough sleep, smoke, wear seat belts, exercise, and so on" (Siegel, p. 66). Choices about such things are statements about how much we care about living.

The good news is that we can learn the skill of loving ourselves once we get beyond learned barriers.

Bad Religion

Bad religion has taught us that it is wrong for us to love ourselves. Such notions are said to be selfish and egotistical, thus sinful. To put it bluntly, that is what we in Southeast Missouri called "Hogwash!" Self-love is the ability to value self appropriately.

The truth is that self-love is at the center of the Christian ethical system. As referenced above, Jesus taught that we are to love our neighbors as *we love ourselves.* He also gave us the "golden rule" which states that we are to do unto others as we would have them *do unto us* (Luke 6:31) . It is clear that self-love is an essential part of the equation in relating to others.

Loving yourself is a source of energy that will empower you to do productive and satisfying things with your life. It will empower you to apply many of the skills you have read about in the preceding chapters. If you love yourself you will be more highly motivated to love others.

Self-love is another way of saying positive self-esteem. Lord knows we need positive self-esteem. Life is difficult enough for those who have it. There is absolutely nothing wrong with loving or valuing yourself.

Think about this. In *Love, Medicine and Miracles*

Siegel writes, "Positive self-adoration remains the essence of health. . . . Self-esteem and self-love are not sinful" (p. 66). Clearly this makes living a joy instead of a chore.

If you don't love yourself you will not be well equipped to love others. The bottom line is that *it is essential to love and be loved.* In fact, even if you are able to apply every principle suggested in this book, but you do not have a sense of being loved, it will be very difficult for you to love truly or live effectively.

Paul wrote in 1 Corinthians 13:1-3 that no matter what good we do, if we do not have love, it all adds up to nothing. We all need love—for ourselves and for others.

Higher Self-Esteem Produces Better Life Habits

A middle-aged woman who was suffering from low self-esteem came to me for help. She was developing some destructive habits in her life but had no sense of motivation to stop them. She was overeating, drinking too much, sleeping too much, and in general becoming depressed. Life was hardly worth living for her.

It seems so simplistic as I look back. We met for several sessions in my office, and in the course of those meetings I made a statement to her in response to her apathy. "I believe that you are better than that."

A few months later she came back, literally bouncing into my office. She was doing well. I knew that she was better when we stopped the formal counseling sessions, but I didn't know whether or not she would continue to improve. She had.

I asked her what had made the most difference for her. She said, "The one statement that really stuck in my mind was when you told me that I was 'better than that.'" Once she began to value herself—to *love herself*—she was able to "start living again."

Once we love ourselves we have the power to love others, and what a difference loving people can make! A boy I will call C. was the foster son of two drug addicts. He had been physically as well as psychologically abused. He regularly sought attention in one of the common ways discouraged people seek attention. He misbehaved. I suspect that C. misbehaved because he believed that getting attention would at least indicate that someone cared about him.

We are not unlike C. We count more, or so we think, if someone is paying attention to us.

The principal in his school observed that the boy's behavior was much worse when there was evidence of physical abuse. One day she found him creating a disturbance in the library. She shook her head and said, "C., what am I going to do with you?"

The boy squirmed a bit and then looked up with his big dark eyes and tried to smile, "Don't do nothing with me. Just love me!" He instinctively knew what he needed. If more of us loved ourselves, we would be better able to help people like this young man. His situation was reported to the authorities, and he was pulled from that foster home, but will he be loved? He will, if he is fortunate enough to be placed in a home of people who value themselves enough to love themselves.

How Can I Learn to Express Love to Myself?

Here are two suggestions for developing this crucial skill.

1. Act in love toward others. Think of people who need to experience love. Take or send them a gift, a cake, some flowers, or even a nice card. If you cannot think of anyone, then call volunteer organizations and ask for suggestions. You can always find people in nursing homes who need someone to express love to them. Make a concentrated effort to find someone who needs your love. You will become healthier, happier, and more productive in the process.

Is there anyone in your life who needs to hear from you? Don't wait. It is vital for them and for you that you visit them, call them, or write them an encouraging note. It will boost your energy.

2. Make a list of all the things you can do to express love to anyone. Select from that list things you can do for yourself. Any experience of love will help you to feel loved, even if you do those things for yourself.

As you are experiencing those things, repeat to yourself, "I am a person who deserves to be loved. I have as much worth and value as anyone in the world."

Verbalize it! "I am loved. I am free to love myself. Loving means that I value myself. I have as much value as anyone in the world. It is mine because I am a human being."

Love is a source of positive energy. To feel loved is to be energized. Love yourself and love others. The value and power of this truth is not a secret, but it is recognized in *The Secret*. "There is no greater power in the Universe than the power of love. The feeling of love is the highest frequency you can emit. If you could wrap every thought in love, if you could love everything and everyone, your life would be transformed" (p. 38).

Memorize it! Say it in terms you can remember. Make them as dramatic and memorable as you can. Ethel Waters said of her worth and value, "God don't make no junk." Maybe you can remember a paraphrase of an old song, "I love me, a bushel and a peck." Write notes to yourself: "Remember, I am loved."

Visualize it! Picture yourself basking in a spa, soaking up warmth and love. See yourself with someone you love. Imagine that you are experiencing that person's love. I used to pick up my little daughter, hold her close, and say, "Do you feel the love flowing from my heart." She said she could! Imagine that you feel love flowing into your heart.

Actualize it! Act in love toward someone and do the things that express love for yourself. Go back to the list of things that express love. Make a plan and set a time to do some of those things this very week.

The Greatest of These Is Love

Remember: Of all the treasures and virtues of life, love is the greatest!

11

What Are We Missing?

Most of us do not like to miss opportunities. My dad was like that. He did not want to miss anything. I once asked him if he was getting enough sleep, and he responded with a grin, "I get too much sleep. I wouldn't sleep at all if I didn't just have to. You never see anything or learn anything while you are asleep. It seems that we miss a lot when we are asleep." I hope he was joking, but I know he really didn't like to miss anything.

His desire to be involved in whatever was happening led him to live a fulfilled life. I listened recently to a taped conversation I had with him on one of our trips together. I asked him if he thought he was successful in life. He said that he believed that he was a very successful person. I wondered how he could come to that conclusion since he was retired and had very little money. He said, "Well, Bill, most people measure their success by how much money they have, but I measure mine by how much fun I have had. I have had a lot of fun in life. There isn't much I would change. I think I am successful." I agreed and dropped the subject but kept his homespun philosophy in my mind.

My dad didn't miss much fun when the opportunity presented itself. I think we miss a lot of fun and a lot of opportunities to live a life that could fulfill our dreams.

Why Do We Miss So Much?

Fear is one culprit. We miss so much of what is possible because we are afraid of the things we don't understand. Our fears block us from experiencing new and exciting things. At the same time fear fills our life with negative results. The reality of this truth came to me through a question, "What would you do if you were not afraid?" Thinking about that question I came to realize that just beyond my mountain of fear is the plain of freedom where I can experience new and exhilarating life. In his book *What Makes the Great Great,* Dennis Kimbro says, "It is fear that is the root cause of negative emotions, unhappiness, and problems in human relationships. The only positive aspect regarding the emotion of fear is that it is learned, and consequently it can be unlearned" (p. 78).

The concepts that we have at our disposal (as verbalized in *The Secret* and in many books on the power of goals) will open doors of opportunity and achievement for us. All we have to do is implement them. There is so much more available to us than we actually experience. It is tragic to think that we miss so much! This was one of the things that motivated me to attempt to draw truth from *The Secret* and apply it in a spiritually consistent way. I hope to alleviate fear from the equation and help others experience the best parts of this philosophy.

It saddens me to realize that because people don't agree with or understand every aspect of a concept, they let their fear of that concept keep them from the benefits they might reap from it.

It Is Not Only Fear That Stops Us

We often miss new things because they are not as easy to apply as their proponents lead us to believe. In fact, any new way of thinking requires effort. We have to break the old patterns of thought in order to embrace new patterns. This requires discipline.

We need the discipline of focus in our life to open our mind to the possibilities that are available to us. I believe that we are meant to live life to its fullest and best levels. The tragedy for so many of us is that we only fill our cup half full. By applying the principles of *The Secret* with the filters and limitations suggested in the chapter on guardrails of the mind, we can fill our cup full.

The Consequences of Missing Possibilities

Can you imagine the dramatic and sad scene at the end of life when people who had great abilities but never made full use of them realize what they "could have been"? Artists grabbing for brushes and paint, writers reaching for pen and paper, musicians stretching for instruments and musical score, and thousands crying for more time will all produce much weeping and wailing. This picture should motivate us to make better use of the gifts we have been given.

The Good News!

We do not have to continue missing the best things in life. We can become what Abraham Maslow called "self actualizing" people. Steven Covey called it being "proactive." Anthony Robbins called it "personal power." It all means that we can become more if we are willing to put into practice what we know to be the best guidelines for fulfillment in our lives. We have been looking at those guidelines throughout the previous pages of this material.

Consider the following question, the answers to which will give us a boost toward applying the best of what we have learned about dreaming our dreams, setting our goals, attracting our destiny, and realizing our potential: *"When do we start practicing what we have learned?"*

Nowness!

There is a skill that can help us answer the question of when to begin practicing what we have learned. I call it the skill of "Nowness." No matter what we have missed up to now, we need miss no more. The answer is simple: *Just do it!* The biggest step we can take in the direction of fulfillment is to stop mulling over or living in the past. Writing of the past Eric Butterworth said, "It came to pass, not to stay."

We miss life by not living in the present. We waste precious time fretting about the lost past. Carl Sandburg said, "I tell you the past is a bucket of ashes." Sandburg was not devaluing or depreciating the past, which is a good place to visit for important lessons or fond memories. He was simply saying that, good or bad, it is gone like wood that has been burned to ashes. Throw it out and start now. L. P. Hartley said, "The past is a foreign country; they do things differently there." Come home to the present.

It is practical to focus on the present; after all, it is all that we really have. The past has made us what we are now. Looking back may be a way to learn some lessons, but it is otherwise useless. Perhaps we made decisions and drew things to us in the past that were not good. We cannot change the past, but we can change the present.

Good or bad, your history is over. The past is a story. It is not you. It is a story about you. The story may be a terrible one. It may be a wonderful one. It is simply not a place to live, and you don't need to continue focusing on it. Let it go and begin now to envision the things that you desire.

Concerning the past, Wally Amos, who had a cookie empire that crumbled, said, "You can't run from it. You can't hide from it. The only thing you can do to make it leave you alone is to accept it." Accept it as a story that happened, and then move on.

Regret and Guilt about the Past Can Jeopardize the Future

Our present is the ground for new dreams and visions. Don't let the past blind you to that fact. Too many of us view ourselves as unworthy for present success because we have done wrong things. Guilt over the past is a waste of energy. It is worthless. In fact, the only valid use of guilt is to avoid future mistakes and to make restitution wherever it is possible.

When I am tempted to fall into the trap of guilt and unworthiness, I remember stories of King David, who certainly was a moral failure but who overcame it to become one of the great kings of Israel. I remember the disciple Simon Peter, who denied Jesus three times but put it behind him and went on to become a great leader in the church. I remember the repeated political failures of Abraham Lincoln, who put them behind him and went on to become a great president.

It is vital to remember that no matter what "has been" it need not be a predictor of what "can be."

Anticipation and Fear of the Future Can Paralyze the Present

The future can be bright, but it too is no place to live. Plan for it and live as if it is going to be everything you dream for it, but live as if today is all that you have. It is! Tomorrow is a promise. Today is real.

We have seen that fear of the future can be as debilitating as regret and guilt about the past. I mention this subject because some of the people with whom I have worked over the last thirty-plus years have literally paralyzed themselves with fear of the future. They fear failure, marriage, children, divorce, rejection, pain, illness, death, etc. They have "crossed those bridges" a thousand times but haven't come to a one of them yet.

No one—not your doctor, not your psychic, not the astrologers, not the fortune-tellers—no one knows the future. That is why you are free to dream it, envision it, and plan for the best.

When Charlie first came into my office he was a very discouraged person. He described his cancer condition as terminal. He told me that he would be on chemotherapy for the rest of his life. He knew that was so because his oncologist (cancer doctor) had told him.

I knew that the situation was serious, but I also knew that no one really knows how one will respond to treatment. I urged him to set some goals, to go ahead and plan a vacation that he and his wife wanted to take. He wanted to do some deep-sea fishing but had always put it off. Now he was reluctant to make such a plan because he couldn't be away from the chemo for that long.

I urged him to remember that anything is possible and that the future is uncertain. He agreed to begin planning.

His is a happy story. He was off chemo in three months. His cancer was in remission. Charlie went on two deep-sea fishing trips and thoroughly enjoyed the last five years of his life. He dared to dream a dream, and it came to pass.

Discipline Is Not a Dirty Word

There are few, if any, free lunches. Discipline is a part of the price we pay for the rewards we want in the future. Self-control is the skill that will enable us to dream and achieve our dreams. Plato said, "The first and best victory is for a man to conquer himself."

Discipline is not popular. We may give lip service to believing it is a good thing. We may even have a discussion about how important it is while indulging ourselves in excessive food or drink or puffing on a cigarette. We may even be able to pass an exam on discipline while still living an undisciplined life. Life, however, cannot be lived effectively without discipline. It is required to get studying done for educational tasks. It is required to get to work on time. It is required to keep records for personal income taxes. It is required to keep a clean house. It is even required in setting aside *time to dream our dreams and set our goals.*

Self-control (which is a characteristic of healthy spirituality) can be achieved if we remember five things:

1. The hard thing is the easiest, and the easy thing is the hardest.

This mind-set has been tremendously helpful to me in sticking to my commitments. It is a clear principle, but one that is often ignored. A few examples will suffice to clarify the concept.

It is hard to keep on studying when others are involved in recreational activity, but when test day comes, the test is easier if we have done the hard thing in advance.

It is easy to join in the recreation and ignore studying, but when the test is given, if we have chosen the easy thing first, the test is harder.

On most days it is hard to follow an exercise program, but when the cardiovascular exam shows that our body is in very good condition, the hard thing has made life easier. It is easy to forget about exercising and watching our diet, but when our body sags and the exams show that our system is clogging up to the point that we may need surgery, the easy thing has become the hardest.

What does discipline have to do with applying the principles of *The Secret*?

We must discipline our mind in order to focus on the things we desire. We need self-control to keep on focusing on the positives and turning our thoughts away from the negatives.

2. To reach our goals we must begin with small approximations. (This concept was introduced in chapter 3.)

It is a principle of behavior modification that we cannot change big behaviors until we have started with small ones. A clear example of a small approximation is found in weight control. If you set a goal of losing thirty pounds you may feel overwhelmed with the challenge. Set an intermediate goal of losing two pounds. You can lose more later, but set a goal that you can reach and begin to feel the joy of success. It will help you to move forward. In other words, don't expect too much from yourself on the first day or week of adding a new discipline to your life.

In applying the principle of believing, in the book *The Secret* it is suggested that we start with the expression of small desires and build up to the larger ones. In developing the practice of believing (faith), the principle of small approximations is valid.

3. We must persist in one area before trying to generalize. We must apply self-discipline to one area of our life at a time. When applying the principle of attracting our desires, we should begin with one area of our life and not try to improve and change everything at one time.

One client told me that he never exercised because he couldn't spend one hour a day achieving a proper workout. When I suggested that he start with fifteen minutes a day, he responded, "No, if I can't do a thing right I just don't want to do it." Every journey begins with a single step, and every house is cleaned one area at a time. Your life can be enriched if you focus on enriching one area at a time. Pick something that you want to improve and begin to visualize that one area at a time.

4. We are all motivated by reward.

In advance of attempting a new area of discipline in

your life think of something that gives you great pleasure, something that you would not ordinarily do for yourself. Plan to do that for yourself after you have successfully practiced a new area of growth in your life.

I envision myself losing weight. I picture in my mind how I will look after I have lost the weight. I set a realistic goal. Suppose I want to lose nine pounds. After I have lost those nine pounds I will treat myself to a trip to Phoenix to visit some of my grandchildren. That adds motivation to my visualization and makes me more likely to follow through with whatever is necessary to reach my goal.

5. *"Never, never, never quit."*

This quote from one of Winston Churchill's commencement addresses has often inspired me. If you are tempted to quit, do it tomorrow, not today. Discipline is a matter of commitment. We can achieve just about anything that we can imagine if we really want to achieve it. We do not lack "will power." We lack "want power." When we want to achieve something badly enough to pay the price through the discipline of visualization, we can do it.

When we begin to hold a vision of our desire or desires in our mind, we must continue it until it becomes second nature to us. Doing it a few times will not achieve much.

When I first began to work with visualizing to improve performance for major league baseball players, I used audiocassette tapes. I would make a tape describing the perfect pitch or the perfect swing of the bat. It began with a section on relaxation and followed with the specific description needed by the player.

One pitcher had an immediate positive response to the tape. After a few weeks he drifted back into his old habits on the mound and told me that the concept was no longer working. I asked him if he was listening to the tape. He said that he had already done that. He listened to it a couple of times a day for two weeks and then stopped.

I told him that the only way it would be effective was for him to listen to it two or three times a day for months. That meant going over the same material, imagining the same process, seeing the same results over and over again. It would at times become boring, but he would have to keep it up in order to get the results he wanted. Once the process had changed his inner belief system, "I am not sure I can throw this pitch over the plate," to the new belief system, "I have perfect control of this pitch," then he could quit listening to the tape.

We develop our beliefs over a long period of time. We repeat them to ourselves hundreds of times. They may have been instilled by the people around us. We heard them say, "Oh, he can't do that," or "She will never be able to get that kind of job." We internalize the things we hear until they become a part of our deep belief system. We always perform or achieve according to our deepest and most consistent beliefs or thoughts. We can only change the outward results by changing the inner beliefs. That does not happen without repeated positive input in the present. It requires discipline and repetition.

We can change our inner beliefs, images, thoughts, visions, and even our wants. It is a simple process, but not an easy one to maintain. When the novelty of a new practice wears off we will continue it only if we are committed to it. We must desire it enough to continue even when we don't see immediate results. Never quit filling your mind with positives. The Bible teaches that we are to control our thoughts and focus them on the things that are good. We noted this in the chapter on guardrails of the mind. This is a spiritually healthy concept.

The idea of changing our "wants" was brought home to me when I heard a counselor say to a client who wanted to quit smoking, "Do you really want to quit?"

The answer was, "Yes, but I just don't have the will power to do it."

The counselor said, "You have all the will power that you need. You just don't have the 'want' power that you need." When asked to explain, the counselor said, "If I gave you one hundred dollars a day for every day that you did not smoke, how many days do you think you could go without a cigarette?"

The client said, "I would imagine I could go for a long time."

"That is true," said the counselor, "and that is because your motivation or 'want' power has been elevated. If it is worth it to you, you can do it. Now think about what it means to quit. You will not be given money, but you will be given stronger lungs and a better chance to avoid cancer. How important is that to you?"

The point was made. Apply that principle to the discipline of spending time identifying your desires, screening them, and practicing focus on them. It all ties together.

Why So Much Focus on Discipline and Follow Through?

I am emphasizing discipline and follow through as a part of the application of the principles of *The Secret* because seldom is anything of value accomplished without effort. It is wonderful to express faith, be positive, and seek to attract your desires, but it will be a shallow experience and not likely to last unless you have been willing to pay the price of effort and follow through to achieve what you desire.

The Importance of Focus

In *The Secret* much is made of the importance of focusing on the things we want and not on the things we do not want. I believe that the skill of positive focus is one of the keys not only to getting things we desire but also in learning to enjoy what we have.

Few people would contradict the notion that a positive outlook is essential for living an effective life. I determine the focus in my own life. So do you. We cannot control the things that happen to us, but we can choose how we will view them. We can also choose the things we want to achieve or obtain and focus on them.

No matter what our focus has been in the past it can be changed. When we change the way we view an event or circumstance it is called "reframing." We don't control all that happens to us, but we do control the frames we put around the pictures of what has happened.

My father, who really did say all the things I credit to him, taught me that the way to be happy was not necessarily to get all that I wanted out of life but to learn to want what I got. That is one kind of positive focus.

He once casually remarked that he did everything he wanted to do. I questioned that statement because I knew there were a lot of things he couldn't afford to do. He applied the principle mentioned above. He said, "I have learned not to want to do what I can't afford to do." That might leave some people a little cold, but I think we could all use a little of that wisdom to replace our insatiable desires for more and more. It isn't a perfect solution, but it is a healthy focus.

The ability to control your focus immediately can raise the level of quality in your life. Note that I am not suggesting that you simply convince yourself that everything in life is positive. I am saying that you can develop the skill of finding the real positive side of whatever is happening or has happened to you.

There Will Be Disappointments

It would be irresponsible to suggest that through positive focus we will get everything we want. That does seem to be the extravagant claim of *The Secret.* We can certainly get a lot more of what we desire, and we can also raise our level of satisfaction with what we do get.

Positive focus puts our attention, not on the event or circumstance, but on the results of the event or circumstance. A salesperson will not make every sale. He will experience some rejection. In and of itself, rejection is not a positive experience, but we can learn and grow through such experiences.

We grow stronger because we are able to see that rejection or failure to get a specific thing that we want is not devastating. It is simply an experience. If we can't handle a little rejection and a few disappointments we will have a struggle in life. Even with the best visualizing, focusing, dreaming, and goal setting, there will be occasional failure. That is all right as long as we learn from the experience and grow through it. Learning and growth are positive experiences.

One seminar leader told a group of us, "I don't always succeed in what I am attempting, but I always succeed in getting a result. It may not be the result I want, but I get a result, and I learn from it. That is what I mean by positive focus, and if you exercise it you will live an effective life, no matter what your outward circumstances."

Epictetus, a Greek Stoic philosopher, summed it up in the first century with these words, "I am upset, not by events, but rather by the way I view them."

This is not a compromise! It is the exercise of our basic right to take what is and make the most of it without complaining. We rise from disappointment to dream anew and continue to pursue our soul's sincere desires.

We generally find the things that we are looking for if we continue looking for them. If we look long enough for a negative consequence we will find it. Conversely, if we look consistently for a positive consequence we will find that.

It doesn't take many negative events to convince the average negative thinker that he is right. Some suggest that it takes several positive statements to offset one negative. It probably takes only one negative event to convince negative people that they are right.

This is pertinent to pursuing the promises of *The*

Secret. One failure does not negate the whole concept. Nor does one positive experience confirm it. I am convinced that we just have to persist in the positive application of the principle in order to reap the benefits of it.

If we are going to find the things for which we are looking, we are going to have to look for the best things in life. This is not unrealistic. It simply means that we are much more likely to find the positives if we consciously and consistently look for them.

If we accentuate the positive, we will certainly reduce the impact of the negative.

Many of Us Have Long Known the Power of Choice

We can choose to dream or not to dream. We can choose to focus on the things we want or on the things we dread. We can choose to blame circumstances for our life, or we can choose to change circumstances into good things.

It is amazing that so many people go through life without the slightest notion that they are making decisions as they go. They seem to think that life just happens to them. Here are some dreams and goals that I choose for my focus.

I choose to focus on life. I picture myself as a healthy person, and my goal is to make decisions that support that picture and goal. I have an elliptical trainer in my exercise room. When I hold in my mind a vision of health and wholeness I begin my day by doing three miles on my trainer. When my actions support my dreams I have a more realistic right to expect fulfillment. It is more than visualizing. It is actualizing.

When my dream is for better health, and it is, I

choose to eat healthier foods. I choose less fat and more fruits and vegetables. I dream of health and then support my dream with my actions. *I firmly believe that unless I am willing to support my dreams with my actions I have no right to expect them to come true.*

The Secret Is in the Open

Successful people know what their dreams are. They have the ability to wrap their minds around their dreams and never let them go. They support their dreams with their actions. When asked when he knew that he wanted to become an attorney, a successful attorney responded, "I have wanted to be a lawyer for as long as I can remember. I looked at other careers but always came back to law." The results of his persistent dream led him to law school after he had finished two other degrees. His mind remained wrapped around his dream.

In public interviews, comedian Jim Carrey has been asked when he began the pursuit of his career in comedy. He has responded to that question by saying that he always wanted to make people laugh. From the time he was a child he performed as the class and family comedian. That goal or dream sustained him during the struggling years as he began the now famous career.

Most highly successful people repeat stories similar to these. It seems that, in Stephen Covey's words, "They began with the end in sight." Even if we don't begin early in life with clear goals and dreams, it is not too late to begin now. We only need to look at the success of chicken king Colonel Sanders to realize that we can begin to dream a dream, even in retirement years. All we have to do is apply the principle. It leads to success.

These three secrets (knowing our dream, holding it in our mind, and acting in ways that support the dream) are available to all of us. They are secrets no longer!

Five Steps to Dream Fulfillment

Begin by *clarifying your dreams.* Usually these are things that are consistent with your personality and gifts. It would be hard to dream of becoming a writer if you have trouble putting sentences together and don't even enjoy that process. Begin by getting in touch with your basic abilities and your personal likes.

Narrow down those things to specific ways to use and fulfill them: How can I best use my abilities? What can I do that I really enjoy? What do I want in life?

Once you identify your dream you would be wise to *run it through the guardrails of the mind.* Read and reread chapter 4 until it becomes deeply imbedded in your mind. It will help you to screen your dreams and goals for the rest of your life.

When you are satisfied that your dream passes the test of things that are true, just, honest, pure, lovely, and of good report, *wrap your mind around that dream and never, never let it go.*

The next step is vital. *Clearly commit yourself to doing whatever it takes to achieve your dream or goal.* Honestly promise yourself that you will support your dream with your actions.

Young people may have a dream of obtaining a college education. In almost all situations that dream will pass the tests of chapter 4. If, as a young person, you wrap your mind around that dream and hold it in your mind and heart every day, the opportunity will come for you to fulfill that dream. The opportunity will present itself to you, but you will have the responsibility of doing whatever it takes to meet the opportunity with your own efforts.

Inspired and encouraged by his older sister, my oldest grandson wanted a college degree. His parents were divorced, and neither of them was prepared to help him. Still, he determined in his heart that he wanted an education. He knew that he would have to work to pay his own way through school. Little help was available to him.

He held his dream in his heart and mind. He *never wavered* from it. The first action that he took was enrolling in college. You can't win a lottery if you don't buy a ticket, and you can't get a college education if you don't enroll. He took the first step.

He worked as a busboy, as a waiter, and as a bartender in order to earn money for tuition, books, room, transportation, and food. He took classes in the day and worked at night. It took him much longer than the four years usually required, but he made it through and now has a degree in marketing. He dreamed his dream and supported his dream with his efforts.

I have no doubt that he will continue to succeed because he has developed a pattern of establishing his goals, sticking to them, and taking the actions that support them.

Most of the material written about success seems to focus on obtaining wealth as the measure of success. That is unfortunate because wealth is only one mark of success, and perhaps not the major one. People who have lived life doing the things that bring fulfillment to them are successful, regardless of the wealth they accumulate.

It is generally true that when we do the things that bring joy and satisfaction to us, we will make a living, and more, as well. Seek and dream of the things you respect and desire for yourself. Dream your own dream and stick to it.

Age, race, and gender must not be permitted to deter our dreams. Thank God, we have made great strides toward reducing the bias and prejudice of those things once considered almost insurmountable.

The racial deterrent was dealt a deathblow by . . . guess who. A man who *"had a dream."* Martin Luther King, Jr., has become a symbol of dreaming a great dream. He did not let threats, abuse, hardships, or even the threat of his life keep him from marching his way to his dream. The result is that millions have benefited from his vision and determination. Now African-Americans are more able than at any time in our history to dream their own dreams and pursue them.

Because heroic women and men of the past have had visions and dreamed their dreams in spite of opposition, we all have the opportunity to pursue goals that were once considered unattainable.

Never, never sell your dreams short. Apply the helpful principles of visualizing your positive future and imagining your successes.

Beyond the Dreams There Must Be Action

John Maxwell says that dreams are first *thought* (imagined), then *caught* (embraced), and next *bought* (attained through effort). Think about your dreams, embrace them with passion, and buy into them with action. The cost is always active pursuit. You have to set your ships afloat. They never achieve your purpose anchored in the harbor of thought and emotion.

Supportive actions are the mark that verifies the integrity of your dream. The supportive actions are sometimes a real challenge. Still, they answer the question, "Do I want my dream enough to pay the price for it?"

I have told you about my dream of attaining a PhD from Washington University in St. Louis. I could have obtained a doctoral degree from less challenging programs. There are institutes, school by mail programs, and degree mills available to those who are unwilling to pay the price for academically acceptable degrees, but my dream included more than just a "degree." I wanted the substance that went with it.

The cost was enormous for me. It took three years of residency (ninety-plus hours of course work), fifteen hundred hours of supervised internship, two days of oral and written exams, seven years of research, a dissertation, and an oral defense of that project. This meant time away from my family and long hours of study. It took almost ten years to complete. I am pleased that I dreamed the dream and paid the price.

Doctors dream of their profession and know at the beginning that in order to realize their dream, they must pay a tremendous price in terms of effort, time, and money. Thousands pay that price. They support their dreams with their actions.

The list goes on. Musicians, carpenters, actors, athletes, mechanics, pilots, marketers, etc. usually have a price to pay in order to reach their goals.

It is spiritually inconsistent to pray for something or dream of something, then expect to receive it without paying the price. Reading a book like *The Secret* may leave some with the impression that all they have to do is set the dream asail and wait for their ship to come in. That is a gross oversimplification, and it is misleading.

Of course there is effort involved in the practice of visualizing and focusing on goals. Studies in visualization reveal that performance, such as shooting free throws, is improved more by spending thirty minutes a day visualizing the action than by actually spending that time practicing. The interesting thing is that visualizing plus practicing raises the level of performance even more. We simply cannot get away from the spiritual law, even the moral law, that outcome is related to effort.

It is true that effort alone will often fall short, but wishing alone will also fall short. It is not a question of either/or but of both/and.

Vision and Action Lead to Results—and the Risk of Change

Overcoming fear has already been mentioned as a factor in personal achievement. That is important because growth and change often, if not usually, involve risk. In order to get over the hurdle, we have to jump. A bird does not learn to fly by sitting in the nest and thinking about flying. It must be pushed into risk taking before flying takes place.

Marriage requires risk. We cannot know everything about a person and how a relationship will work out unless we are willing to take the risk of commitment. Frequently while one man is hesitating until he gets more information, the woman marries a man who loves her enough to run the risk of commitment.

Life always involves risks. Productive and fulfilling life involves even more risks. At some point precaution must meet with action or nothing will be achieved.

Can't I Just Take a Pill?

Reaching our goals and realizing our dreams require us to grow, and growth means change. That is a process that usually takes time. We Americans are not known for our great patience. We have become a nation of the quick fix. We don't want to improve our health by changing our lifestyle. We would rather take some kind of pill every day for the rest of our lives than to make the effort to solve the problem. Diabetics want to be able to eat the same foods that they have always eaten, even if it means extra insulin shots or other medication. Cut out the heavy fat content and reduce the sugar? "I'd rather take a pill."

Weight reduction is a multimillion-dollar industry because paying the price of less caloric intake and more physical activity is hard. As hard as it is for many people, even those who do have the capacity to lose weight reasonably often say, "I don't want to cut back my calories and increase my exercise. I would rather take a pill." And how about the athlete who wants a shortcut to muscle mass rather than the laborious weight program? "Just let me take a pill, a steroid, if you please."

Pills are seldom the solution. Some conditions require medication. There is no question about that, but others do not. Still, we would rather be pill poppers than life changers.

Make Patience Part of Your Plans

Application of the principles that bring dreams into reality is possible for anyone. These principles work. The problem is that there are actions that make them work, and these actions are often overlooked. After you have specified your dream, run it through the guardrails of the mind, exercised the discipline of focus, and added supportive actions, you may still have to patiently and persistently wait for fulfillment.

Fulfillment of some of your dreams may take months and even years. There is no "quick and easy" method for reaching your goals, but you can reach them. If it is worth it, pursue it.

I have shared some of my past dreams. I knew what I wanted. They were dreams that were true to my deepest commitments, and I was willing to support them with my actions. Some of them were fulfilled within a few years, but others took as much as twenty to thirty years for fulfillment. Persistently dreaming and waiting resulted in fulfillment.

This fact is mentioned here because many charlatans would lead you to believe that your goals can be reached with no effort and within a matter of a few days at most. This is simply not true. But the truth will set you free (John 8:32) to pursue your dreams without stumbling over unrealistic expectations. As George Matthews Adams says, no dream comes true automatically; we have to buy it. We must pay a price for our dreams and visions. A large part of that price includes self-control (self-discipline) to commit ourselves to achieving our goals.

12

Conclusions

While loving and applying most of what I have read in *The Secret,* I still have a major reluctance to wholesale acceptance of the generalizations made concerning it. The words that are red flags to me are words like "always," "never," "anything," "ever," and "nothing."

Should Christians Question Anything in *The Secret?*

In the following paragraphs I list two important principles in *The Secret* that Christians need to question because they are misleading or inaccurate.

1. We attract everything that comes into our lives.

When I read a statement like, "Nothing can ever come into your life that you do not attract," I back away. I certainly acknowledge that a great deal, even perhaps most, of what comes into our lives may be attracted by our thoughts and desires. We may, like magnets, attract much of what we experience, *but not everything* that we experience.

Some things come into our lives that we do not attract. Consider the following example.

The precious young couple sit weeping before me. They are as devout and good as any people I have known, and I know this couple very well. They have just received news that their newborn is a Down syndrome baby. I cannot for the life of me imagine anyone looking into their distressed faces and declaring, "Nothing comes into your experience that you did not attract."

Surely the general truth of attraction cannot apply to every situation.

My telephone rang at 4:00 A.M. It was a rainy night in early spring. The voice on the other end was almost unintelligible. "Bill," he sobbed, "they've both been killed." His wife and only son had driven onto an unmarked railroad crossing. They were hit by a train and killed instantly.

She was an office worker in the church and a faithful Christian. There was no way then, or ever, that I would tell that young man, "Nothing comes into your life that you did not draw into it by your thoughts and feelings."

I embrace the sense of hope and responsibility that the concept of attraction brings to thousands of people, but I cannot embrace the absolutist language that can be devastating to many others. There must be exceptions to that "law." Those exceptions do not go without saying. We must verbalize them for those who will be crushed by an apparent encouraging word that becomes a living horror for them.

2. We receive everything that we want.

The second idea that gives me pause is the statement that we receive everything that we want when we apply the principles taught in *The Secret.* We may receive much of what we want. We may receive more than we ever thought possible, but seldom, if ever, will we receive *everything* that we want.

The message in the Jim Carrey movie *Bruce Almighty* should make it clear how chaotic it would be if we were able to fulfill all our requests.

Not only that, but this teaching is also a potential discouragement to people who have their hopes raised to new heights, only to be dashed when they do not receive all that they want. After all, the testimonies they have heard from stupendously successful people who are rich beyond their wildest dreams suggest that if they do not receive the same things, something must be wrong with them. At the very least these empty-handed wishers are not properly and consistently applying the principles. Such people will become more than doubters of principles that could be wonderfully helpful to them—if properly understood and applied. In despair, they may throw out all the teachings instead of continuing to apply what could enrich their lives.

Proponents, though they may have come from impoverished backgrounds, who are now highly successful have more than a tacit responsibility for presenting their "truth" with balance. Otherwise, what is intended as a benefit becomes a burden.

Can Christians Apply Anything in *The Secret?*

Should Christians be reluctant to apply any of the teachings of *The Secret* in their lives? Absolutely not! I only encourage the use of the limitations that I have suggested in this material.

Do these principles work? Yes they do. They do not work one hundred percent of the time, but they always make life better for the people who practice them. What are some of these principles?

1. There is attractive power in our lives.

John Maxwell, mentioned earlier, suggests that not only do individuals attract things into their lives, organizations also attract people who fit their mold of management. They usually do so on a subconscious level, but they attract them just the same.

It seems clear that there is an attraction power in the world. Negatives attract negatives. Positives attract positives. I believe in positive focus, because I also believe in the power of attraction.

2. There is abundance in the universe.

Is there abundance in our world? There certainly is. I only point out that this fact does not liberate us from the responsibility of good stewardship. I believe in the conservation of our resources for generations to come. The same world that is filled with abundance is filled with abundant ways to conserve what we have.

There is enough to go around if we would only learn to share it.

3. The principle of asking is universal.

Should we ask for the things we deeply desire? Yes, I believe so. I do however believe that it is wise to use the guardrails suggested in this material to cleanse and strengthen our deepest desires.

4. We need to be open to truth.

You and I will never rise above our own self-beliefs unless we are willing to examine truth wherever we find it. Let's be willing to raise the ceiling. There is no way of knowing how far we can fly until we spread our wings. We must be able to wrap our mind around the truth of the world if we expect the world to open its mind to the truth we share. The truth will set us free.

As Christians we can read, watch, and apply the basic teachings of *The Secret* without fear of compromising our own convictions. We can do so without becoming our own "gods." We accept God as God, who gives guidance to our lives. We can filter the ideas through our own values and faith.

5. We should keep sending out positives.

I have for many years stood on the back deck of my home and prayed. I sometimes stand there remembering the suggestion of *The Secret* that I am like a radio tower, broadcasting my thoughts and prayers. I think of myself as sending out signals to the world. They are positive signals. They are thoughts and visualizations of health, abundance, creativity, peace, love, and joy. As I "transmit" those thoughts, I perceive them not only as radio waves, but also as prayers.

6. We should keep on giving thanks.

Part of the "transmission" is gratitude. I express thanks for all that I have received. I can do so with the faith that God, the creator of the universe, and not the universe itself, is the source of all that comes into my life.

7. We should not lose our balance.

The fact that some become so enthusiastic about what they perceive as "new" truth, that they push it beyond the boundaries of my values at times, does not keep me from continuing and adding to my own understanding of those truths. I understand how passion about a personal discovery can impel people to extremes. I believe that has at times happened to the people who embrace *The Secret.* It is challenging to grasp a new insight and not lose one's balance.

This Is Not New Material, But It Is Often Overlooked

There is nothing really secret or new about this material. For instance, there is nothing new about visualization. It is as old as the ancient Greeks, to which *The Secret* at times refers. There is nothing new about the concept of positive input. It certainly is a part of Christian heritage and has found voice in many great teachers.

Glen Clark verbalized many of these "secrets" in books like *The Man Who Tapped the Secrets of the Universe,* in which he shared the philosophies of Walter Russell. He shared other truths about bringing together inner thoughts and outer expression of prayer in books like *The Soul's Sincere Desire, How to Find Health Through Prayer,* and *I Will Lift Up Mine Eyes.* I recommend any of these for those who want to see some of these same concepts from a strong Christian point of view.

The Power of Your Subconscious Mind by Joseph Murphy was the first of many books that influenced my thinking about my own mental power.

The Secret is another book that I will keep and use. It certainly has added to my beliefs about the powers God has placed in my being.

Do not be afraid of new ideas. Jesus repeatedly told His disciple to "fear not." When our personal security is found in our relationship to God and our experience of Him, we are free to examine truth wherever it is found and at the same time, without apology, remain committed to our basic faith.

Conclusion

My conclusion about *The Secret* is that it is interesting to read and that it contains a lot of material that can be helpful. I have applied most of the principles taught in the book to my own life. I read it as I attempt to read any book—with an open mind, but not with blinders on.

I encourage you to read *The Secret.*, but I caution that you should read it with an awareness that you need to filter out many of the generalizations in it. Take what is true and helpful to you and accept responsibility for what you apply in your life. I believe the guardrails will help.

So with those guardrails firmly in place, relax, enjoy the concepts, and continue to enrich your life.

Bibliography

Barclay, William. *The Letters to the Philippians, Colossians, and Thessalonians.* Louisville: Westminster Press, 1975.

Byrne, Rhonda. *The Secret.* New York: Atria Books, 2006.

———*The Secret* (DVD). New York: Atria Books, 2006.

Clark, Glenn. *The Man Who Tapped the Secrets of the Universe.* St. Paul: Macalester Park, 1946.

———*The Soul's Sincere Desire.* Boston: Little and Brown, 1953.

Collins, Francis. *The Language of God.* New York: Free Press, 2006.

Kimbro, Dennis. *What Makes the Great Great.* New York: Doubleday, 1998.

Little, Bill L. *Help Yourself Heal: 8 Steps to Health & Wholeness.* Minneapolis: Comp/Care, 1990.

———*Prevention: The Ultimate Cure.* Gretna, LA: Pelican Publishing, 2006.

Luthe, W. *Autogenic Therapy,* vol. II. New York: Grune and Stratton, 1969.

Maxwell, John C. *The 21 Indispensable Qualities of a Leader.* Nashville, TN: Thomas Nelson Publishers, 1999.

Murphy, Joseph. *The Power of Your Subconscious Mind.* Englewood Cliffs, NJ: Prentice-Hall, 1963.

Samuels, Mike and Nancy H. Samuels, *Seeing with the Mind's Eye.* New York: Random House, 1975.

Schultz J. and W. Luthe. *Autogenic regulation training and sickness absence,* cited in the *Journal of Advanced Nursing,* vol. 9, issue 6, 581-87.

Seigel, Bernie. *Love, Medicine and Miracles.* New York: Harper and Row, 1986.

Simonton, O. Carl and Stephanie Matthews Simonton, *Getting Well Again.* Los Angeles: J. P. Tarcher, 1978.